Thank you to Kevin Ward for bringing the stories to life with your fine illustrations. Thank you to Jessica Woollard and to everyone at Templar for all your hard work in turning my vague ideas into a proper book. I had naively hoped that writing an illustrated book would be very easy. I was wrong.

My lasting gratitude go to all the adventurers featured in these pages. You have inspired and illuminated my life, and that has made all the difference.

For my Godson, Paddy.
This is a book full of wild, madcap adventurers, their daft exploits and dubious career paths. I commend them all to you as role models. – A.H.

To my fellow adventurer, Oliver. – K.W.

REFERENCES

Note: The publishers have undertaken every effort to ensure information provided is accurate and up-to-date at the time of publication.

p11, 12 Cherry-Garrard, A (Originally published 1922), *The Worst Journey in the World: Antarctic Journey 1910-1913, Volume I+II*, Penguin

p15 Earhart, A Quoted in *Last Flight*, (1937) Harcourt

p20 Lee, L (Originally published 1969) *As I Walked Out One Midsummer Morning*, Andre Deutsch

p21 Hubert. Sheet of Music image. Shutterstock. Web. 24 April 2018.

p23 Manson, A (2012) *Roll On: Rick Hansen Wheels Around the World*, Greystone Books

p29 Murphy, D (1965) *Full Tilt: Ireland to India with a Bicycle*, Overlook Press

p33 The Telegraph article (13 Feb 2005), source available here: https://www.telegraph.co.uk/finance/2905689/Fiennes-tuning-for-executives.html

p39 Bailey, B (1963) Quoted in *Famous Modern Explorers*, Dodd, Mead & Company, New York

p43 Collins, M (Originally published 2001) *Carrying the Fire: An Astronaut's Journey*, Cooper Press

p47 Davidson, R (2012) *Tracks*, Bloomsbury

p51 Kimber, W (1952) *No Picnic on Mount Kenya*, William Kimber

p57 (Outen, S personal communication with the author March 2018)

p61 Hansen, V and Curtis, K.R. Wadsworth (2013) Quoted in *Voyages in World History, Volume I, Brief Edition*, Cengage Learning. Original source *The Travels of Ibn Battuta A.D. 1395-1354*, The Hakluyt Society

P65 (Sherpa, R.L personal communication with the author November 2016)

p69 Bly, N (Originally published 1890) *Around the World in Seventy-Two Days*, Pictorial Weeklies

p73 Thesiger, W (Originally published 1959) *Arabian Sands*, Longmans, London

p77 Sutherland, A (2012) *Paddling North*, Patagonia

p81 Source available here: http://www.benedictallen.com/his-philosophy

p85 Marcovitz, H (2013) Quoted in *Explorers of New Worlds: Sacagawea*, Chelsea House, Infobase Learning

p89 Heyerdahl, T, (Originally published in English, 1950) *The Kon-Tiki Exhibition: By Raft Across the South Seas*, George Allen & Unwin Ltd. 1950

BIG PICTURE PRESS

This edition first published in the UK in 2019 by Big Picture Press.
First published in the UK in 2018 by Big Picture Press,
an imprint of Kings Road Publishing, part of Bonnier Books UK,
The Plaza, 535 King's Road, London, SW10 0SZ
www.templarco.co.uk/big-picture-press
www.bonnierbooks.co.uk

Text copyright © 2018 by Alastair Humphreys
Illustration copyright © 2018 by Kevin Ward
Design copyright © 2018 by Kings Road Publishing Limited

1 3 5 7 9 10 8 6 4 2

ISBN 978-1-78370-841-3 (Hardback)
ISBN 978-1-78741-626-0 (Paperback)
ISBN 978-1-78741-442-6 (E-book)

This book was typeset in True Crimes, Lunchbox Slab and Saturday Sans ICG.
The illustrations were drawn in ink and black watercolour and coloured digitally.

Printed in China

GREAT ADVENTURERS

Alastair Humphreys
Illustrated by Kevin Ward

B P P

MEET THE ADVENTURERS

ALASTAIR HUMPHREYS: P.8
A National Geographic Adventurer of the Year, Alastair is also the author of this book!

APSLEY CHERRY-GARRARD: P.10
Cherry went to Antarctica as an expedition scientist.

AMELIA EARHART: P.14
The first woman to fly solo across the Atlantic Ocean. Amelia later mysteriously disappeared.

BERYL MARKHAM: P.14
A celebrated aviation pioneer, Beryl successfully flew solo across the Atlantic from east to west.

LAURIE LEE: P.18
Setting out one midsummer morning, Laurie walked the length of Spain.

RICK HANSEN: P.22
Paralympian Rick wheeled around the world and inspired a number one hit.

DERVLA MURPHY: P.28
Dervla dreamed about cycling to India for 20 years before she was finally able to go.

RANULPH FIENNES: P.32
Revered explorer Ranulph's longest expedition lasted three years.

JACQUES PICCARD: P.38
Deep-sea adventurer Jacques visited the deepest point on Earth.

MICHAEL COLLINS: P.42
One of the first people to fly to the moon, Michael was part of the historic Apollo 11 mission.

ROBYN DAVIDSON: p.46

Robyn spent years training for her six-month camel trek across the Australian outback.

FELICE BENUZZI: p.50

Prisoner-of-war Felice escaped from jail to climb Mount Kenya.

SARAH OUTEN: p.56

Once the youngest woman to row solo across an ocean, Sarah has travelled around the world.

IBN BATTUTA: p.60

Epic explorer Ibn Battuta visited more countries than Marco Polo.

LAKPA RITA SHERPA: p.64

Mountain guide Lakpa has climbed the highest peak on Earth an astonishing 17 times.

NELLIE BLY: p.68

Determined Nellie Bly travelled around the world in just 72 days.

WILFRED THESIGER: p.72

In unbearable heat and conditions, Wilfred crossed the Empty Quarter desert.

AUDREY SUTHERLAND: p.76

Audrey was 59 when she set out on her first adventure — paddling the Alaskan coastline.

BENEDICT ALLEN: p.80

Solo explorer Benedict once crossed the Amazon basin at its widest point.

SACAGAWEA: p.84

At just 16, Sacagawea led the famous Lewis and Clark Expedition across America.

THOR HEYERDAHL: p.88

Setting sail on a makeshift raft, Thor drifted across the Pacific Ocean to reach the islands of Polynesia.

ADVENTURER UNKNOWN: p.92

This young explorer-in-the-making has a world of opportunities before them.

WE ALL NEED HEROES

HOWEVER YOUNG OR OLD WE ARE.

Heroes who inspire us, make us dream and dare us to try a little harder. Most of my heroes are adventurers. This book tells the stories of their daring feats and epic journeys.

When I was a child, I used to wish that I could head off like my heroes in search of new experiences and a life packed with excitement. To my surprise, I eventually did just that. Made bold by the likes of Dervla Murphy and Ibn Battuta, I left normal life behind and jumped onto my bike. I spent four years cycling round the world, having exactly the sort of adventures that my heroes wrote about. That journey changed my life.

I have met many people who have regretted *not* going on an adventure in their life, but I have *never* met someone who was sorry that they did.

Since cycling round the world I have been on many more exciting expeditions. Enchanted by Laurie Lee's

> " Spending your life doing what you love is a magical privilege – another reason to follow the path of your heroes. "

writing, I followed his footsteps through Spain, playing music on the streets for spare change. I have trekked through the scorching silence of the Empty Quarter desert in Arabia, like Wilfred Thesiger, copied Thor Heyerdahl in crossing a huge ocean in a tiny boat, and even applied to be an astronaut like Michael Collins. I failed the very first intelligence tests, but I'm still glad I gave it a shot!

I don't pretend that my trips matched up to their famous tales, but the connections were still special for me. Over time, Ranulph Fiennes' and Benedict Allen's careers made me believe that I might also turn my passion into my job. And I have – I am an adventurer and a writer. Sometimes I feel lucky. At other times, I just feel I chose the right path.

In this book, I introduce the feats of my adventure heroes. They are some of the most impressive, eccentric, inspiring explorers who ever lived. So many adventurers have made an impact on my life that I am sorry not to be able to include them all. When a character in this book catches your imagination, I hope you will explore further and find out more about their experiences and personalities. The final selection of heroes spans 700 years. They range from teenagers to pensioners and famous to

"You do not need to be extraordinary or a genius to go on an adventure. You simply have to go."

obscure, undertaking their journeys across continents (and oceans and space) by bike, boat and boot, as well as camel, ski, wheelchair and even high-tech machine.

I read a lot of books when I was young, spending long winter afternoons sitting with my back against the warm radiator in my bedroom, or sneaking a few extra pages with my torch under the blankets at night. I hope you enjoy reading this book as much as I enjoyed the stories of my childhood, that the adventurers become your heroes too, and that perhaps one day it sets in motion an adventure of your own.

Through chasing a life of adventure myself, I have learned an important lesson. I now understand my heroes are normal people like you and me. The heroes in this book are just ordinary men and women who decided not to live ordinary lives. I admire them even more for that.

I dearly hope that their stories will encourage you, whatever your age, to think more boldly, go a little further, and live more adventurously yourself.

Alastair Humphreys

APSLEY CHERRY-GARRARD

In an Antarctic winter, even the days are dark. The sub-zero temperatures are brutal. It was into this grim world that three friends set out to try to collect a penguin's egg. Apsley Cherry-Garrard was the youngest member of Captain Scott's famous final expedition. Everyone called him Cherry. The penguin eggs would be useful to scientists, but little did Cherry know that he was about to experience the worst journey in the world.

| wool underwear | wool underlayer | wool hat and scarf | windproof smock | windproof trousers and strong boots | ankle wrappings | fur gloves (attached for safety) |

Cherry wore seven layers to keep warm in sub-zero temperatures.

In ferocious winds of up to 100 km/h, Cherry and his teammates Bill and Birdie battled their way for five weeks across the emptiness of Antarctica. With two big sleds to carry their tent, sleeping bags, food and scientific equipment, they pulled an enormous weight behind them. They either hauled both sleds tied together, or pulled them one at a time when the going was hard.

To make matters worse, the sun never rises during an Antarctic winter and torches had not yet been invented, so they travelled in almost total darkness. Their clothes were coated in ice, and their reindeer-fur sleeping bags froze so hard that it was a struggle to get into them each night. Temperatures dropped as low as –60°C, but despite this, the men never stopped being kind to each other.

BUTTER AND BISCUITS
The perilous trek through the snow and ice from Scott's base to the penguin colony at Cape Crozier took 19 days. On the way, the men plunged into crevasses and Cherry's teeth chattered so much they shattered!

The only food they had was pemmican, biscuits, butter and tea. Pemmican is a mixture of meat, fat, fruit and salt that has been dried into a hard brick. Cherry and his friends ate the same food for every meal of the expedition. They heated snow until it turned into hot water, then stirred in pemmican, butter and crumbled biscuits. They called this meal 'hoosh'.

A NEAR MISS
The team had managed to collect just a few eggs when calamity struck. Their tent blew away in a fierce gale! With no protection against the biting cold, they were almost certain to die. Trapped by the storm, the men spent two days and nights laying in their sleeping bags, shivering and covered in snow.

Once the blizzard passed, they made a desperate attempt to find their tent, even though they were convinced it must have blown out to sea. They were very frightened. However, luck was on their side and Birdie found their tent less than a kilometre away, jammed among some rocks. With great relief, the friends climbed inside to cook some warm hoosh, their first food in days. They were alive!

THE WORST JOURNEY
It truly was the worst journey imaginable, but Cherry, Bill and Birdie survived. The three eggs they brought back are considered extremely precious specimens and you can still see one of them today at the Natural History Museum in London, UK.

When Cherry returned home, he wrote a book called *The Worst Journey in the World*. In it he said, "I think the happiest moment of my life was when we returned safely to the hut. It was warm and light once again. We ate bread and jam, drank hot chocolate, and then climbed into a warm, dry sleeping bag. Within seconds we fell asleep. I was ready to sleep ten thousand years..."

" Our lives had been taken away and given back to us."

THE WORST JOURNEY

Cherry, Bill and Birdie left Captain Scott's base camp and set out on a dangerous journey to the emperor penguin colony. Collecting the eggs and getting them safely back to base was going to be a lot harder than they could ever have imagined...

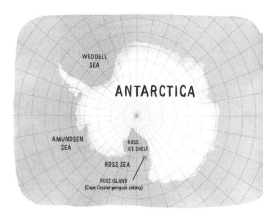

Hey, look! I've got two more!

NOooo!

Yuck!

Don't worry Cherry! Three out of five eggs isn't bad!

WITH THE THREE EGGS PACKED UP THE MEN PREPARED TO RETURN TO BASE.

THEY CHECKED THEIR SLED AS THE WIND WAS GETTING STRONGER...

THEN DISASTER STRUCK...

No! The tent!

> " On the whole, it is better to be a little over-bold than a little over-cautious. "

KIT

Living in total darkness in icy conditions must have been like camping inside a freezer! It was essential that the men had plenty of food, and also candles, so that they could see and keep a little warmer.

BIRDIE, BILL AND CHERRY

1. blubber cooker
2. knife
3. biscuits
4. pemmican
5. candle
6. ice axe
7. penguin eggs
8. tea
9. spirit candle
10. lamp box
11. sleeping bag
12. tent

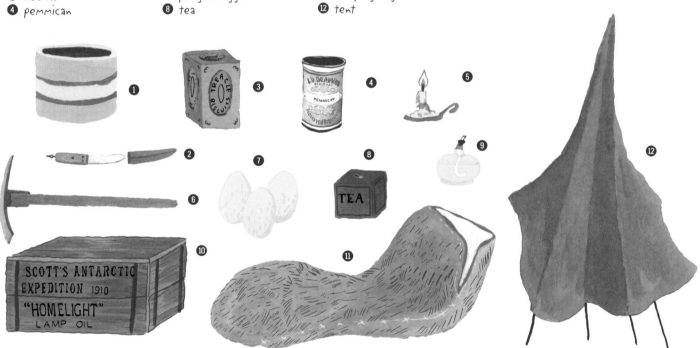

SCOTT'S ANTARCTIC EXPEDITION 1910 "HOMELIGHT" LAMP OIL

TEA

PEMMICAN

Why Apsley Cherry-Garrard Inspired Me

When I first began dreaming of adventures, I thought that explorers were superheroes. But Cherry was a normal person, just like me. He had never been on an expedition before. He was not very strong and he had bad eyesight. So what did he have? He had enthusiasm. I was enthusiastic, too! He was eager to learn and work hard. Me too! Maybe I could go on amazing adventures after all, just like Cherry.

AMELIA EARHART

The first woman to fly solo across the Atlantic Ocean, Amelia's flight made her famous. She was given many awards, including the Distinguished Flying Cross and the Legion of Honour. However, on a later adventure, she disappeared over the Pacific Ocean and neither her body nor plane were ever found.

BERYL MARKHAM

A British-born Kenyan aviator, adventurer, racehorse trainer and author, Beryl was the first woman to successfully fly solo across the Atlantic from east to west. Several women had died trying. Strong headwinds made the westward trip more difficult than east-bound flights. Beryl was celebrated as an aviation pioneer.

> **"The stars seemed near enough to touch and never before have I seen so many. I had always believed the lure of flying is the lure of beauty, but I was sure of it that night."**

It was watching a stunt pilot at a local air show that made Amelia Earhart fall in love with flying. After her first trip in a plane, she knew she had to learn to fly. Searching for adventure, Amelia took off from Newfoundland towards Paris, France. But just three hours into the flight, a serious problem occurred. The altimeter failed, so she had no way of knowing how high she was flying. Shortly afterwards she flew through a dangerous thunderstorm.

After battling through many mechanical problems and icy conditions, she was forced to land, after 15 hours, in a field in Northern Ireland. But she had succeeded!

Amelia later attempted to become the first woman to fly round the world, but her plane went missing over the Pacific Ocean and she was never seen again.

Beryl Markham grew up in a wealthy family in Kenya. She loved hunting barefoot with the local African children, clutching spears and chasing animals through the bush. When she was older, Beryl flew solo across the Atlantic, west with the night, something that no woman had done before.

Taking off from England and heading to New York, Beryl flew a lonely 20-hour flight across the ocean against the wind. With no sleep and only coffee and chicken sandwiches to keep her going, her fuel tanks iced up and she crash-landed in a peat bog in Cape Breton, Nova Scotia, Canada. It wasn't quite the triumphant landing in New York she had hoped for, but a safe first crossing of the Atlantic Ocean nonetheless!

Why Amelia Earhart and Beryl Markham Inspired Me

Amelia Earhart's glamorous life and mysterious disappearance are fascinating. I love her bold advice of "Never interrupt someone doing something you said couldn't be done."

I first read Beryl Markham's book when I was cycling through Africa, where she lived, on my way round the world. I was so inspired that I even named my bicycle 'Beryl'!

LAURIE LEE

Laurie Lee waved goodbye to his mum and walked out one midsummer morning to explore the world. Knowing only one sentence of Spanish, Laurie decided to walk across Spain, playing his violin to earn money along the way. It was his first trip abroad.

You too could know as much Spanish as Laurie at the start of his adventure –

"Un vaso de agua, por favor."

"A glass of water, please."

At 19 years old, young Laurie left his home in Gloucestershire, UK carrying his violin in a blanket, a spare shirt, a torch and a rucksack with some food. He ate his biscuit supply within hours of leaving home! Sleeping in a ditch in the rain on his very first night away made Laurie miserable and he was tempted to go home, but he knew that his brothers would tease him for giving up so soon. So, with a sigh, Laurie kept going and soon cheered up. What would you have done if you were in the same position?

MUSIC AND MERRIMENT

Laurie felt so embarrassed the first time he played his violin in public. He wandered around for ages looking for a good spot to play. Eventually he paused under a bridge and decided it was time to start earning some money. Laurie was nervous but, to his surprise he didn't get arrested and nor did anyone tell him to stop playing. In fact, nobody took any notice at all! Then an old man, without stopping, dropped a coin into Laurie's upturned hat. His first donation – it seemed too easy! Laurie was thrilled because he now knew that wherever he went, he would be able to earn money from busking.

Spain's villages were very quiet so the arrival of a young Englishman with his violin caused a lot of excitement. In the evenings, the locals would ask Laurie to play and the streets were soon filled with dancing, music and laughter – all thanks to his violin.

TOUGH TIMES

On his first night in Spain, Laurie sheltered as best he could out of the wind. He laid his violin beside him, used his rucksack as a pillow and stretched out on a bed of stones. Not only was he extremely uncomfortable, Laurie was woken by snarling wild dogs! Fortunately his camping skills improved and Laurie came to love spending warm nights sleeping under the stars. It was a very simple adventure.

It took Laurie over a year to walk from Vigo in Galicia, to Andalusia in southern Spain. Galicia is known as the land of a thousand rivers and Laurie often swam in the deep, clear pools. With no hat to shield him from the ferocious Spanish heat, he suffered a great deal from sunburn and sometimes even caught sunstroke. Luckily, kind strangers always helped him out with shelter or drinks of water. When he was tired of walking, Laurie sometimes hitched rides to the next town on the back of donkey carts.

HEADING HOME

As he travelled south, past the Roman aqueduct in Segovia and the capital city of Madrid, Laurie heard rumours that war was on its way. By the time he reached the south coast of Spain, Laurie's violin had fallen to pieces and the war had begun. It was time for him to return home.

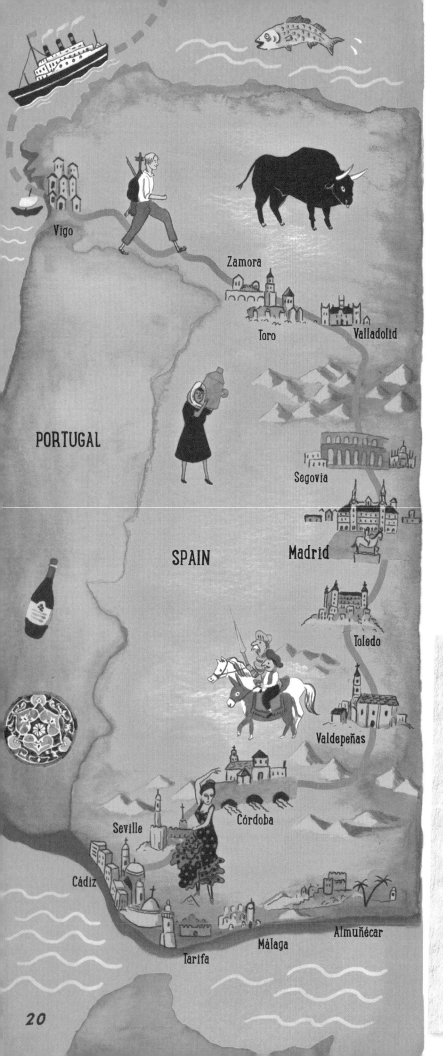

PORTUGAL

Vigo

Zamora

Toro

Valladolid

Segovia

SPAIN

Madrid

Toledo

Valdepeñas

Córdoba

Seville

Cádiz

Tarifa

Málaga

Almuñécar

> **"** I felt for this I had come: to wake at dawn on a hillside and look out on a world for which I had no words, to start at the beginning, speechless and without a plan, in a place that still had no memories for me.**"**

Why Laurie Lee Inspired Me

As I Walked Out One Midsummer Morning is my favourite book. It taught me to travel slowly and live simply. Laurie Lee shaped the style of my own journeys. I was scared to play music in public, but after learning the violin for just seven months, I decided to follow in Laurie's footsteps. The embarrassment of playing in public, the worry of having no money, the kindness of strangers, the wonderful landscapes, the cold river swims: my own brilliant experiences were so similar to Laurie's many years earlier.

DEAR DIARY

August 4th

This morning I woke up, nibbled some bread and fruit, rolled my things into a bundle, and washed my head and feet in a spring. I am very fit now — long walks make everyone strong — and I can walk 30 km a day. It seems ages ago that I was working on a building site in London. I remember looking up at the sky one morning and suddenly realising that I could go anywhere. The only thing stopping me from beginning an adventure was myself.

So where should I go? All I had to do was get there. France? Italy? Greece? I knew nothing about any country. Then I remembered that I had learned a sentence in Spanish and it was this that made my decision. I was heading to Spain.

Now I've followed this track south for days, living on figs and ears of wheat. Sometimes I hide from the sun under the wayside trees, face downwards watching the ants. There is no hurry.

For hour after hour on the plains I saw nothing at all. It was so hot! My feet are scorched and blistered. It took me two days to cross the Sierra de Guadarrama mountains. I climbed upwards along a Roman road built two thousand years ago. Clouds rolled down from the summits and the air smelled fresh. After the heat of the plains it felt like heaven! I have never felt so alive and so alone before.

Laurie

RICK HANSEN

Rick Hansen was just 15 when a car crash on the way home from a fishing trip changed his life forever. He became paralysed from the waist down and would spend the rest of his life in a wheelchair. Before his injury, Rick had daydreamed about cycling round the world, but now he dreamed up an even harder adventure.

Rick is the only adventurer in this book to have a number-one song written about him — St. Elmo's Fire (Man in Motion). That's pretty cool!

Determined not to let his accident stop him, Rick went on to become a successful wheelchair athlete. From completing wheelchair marathons to winning world titles, he even competed at two Paralympics, winning six medals.

Rick began thinking about attempting a huge journey that would help raise money to search for a cure for spinal injury. Well, you can't get any bigger than going round the world on a 40,000-km journey to 34 different countries!

POWERFUL MESSAGE

As well as being a huge adventure, Rick's journey also showed the world that people of all abilities could live adventurously and were important members of their community. It certainly worked – 800,000 people welcomed his arrival in Beijing, China. Rick went on to meet the Pope, and the Prime Minister of Canada dropped a cheque for $1 million into the charity bucket!

A HELPING HAND

Even small tasks like putting up a tent become more difficult in a wheelchair, so Rick picked a team to help him complete his journey. They travelled behind his wheelchair in a motorhome. One of the tour team, Amanda, later became Rick's wife. A fairy-tale ending!

HERO'S WELCOME

During the adventure, Rick had to battle challenges such as scorching deserts, freezing snowstorms and massive mountains. He averaged an exhausting 30,000 wheelchair strokes a day. On top of all that, Rick also had to cope with people who didn't understand what he was doing and did not always treat disabled people kindly.

Despite the hardships, Rick's adventure raised many millions for charity. He returned to Canada to a hero's welcome of huge crowds and a sea of yellow ribbons and balloons.

" There is nothing you can't do if you set your mind to it. Anything is possible. "

Rick is a three-time Paralympic gold medalist.

Why Rick Hansen Inspired Me

I learned about Rick when I cycled through his hometown whilst on my own journey round the world. I was pretty proud of myself for cycling so far until I learned that a paralysed man had done it in a wheelchair! In response to Rick's journey, the people of Canada lined the roads to watch him cycle past and donated huge amounts of money to his charity.

It united the nation and showed everyone the potential of people with disabilities.

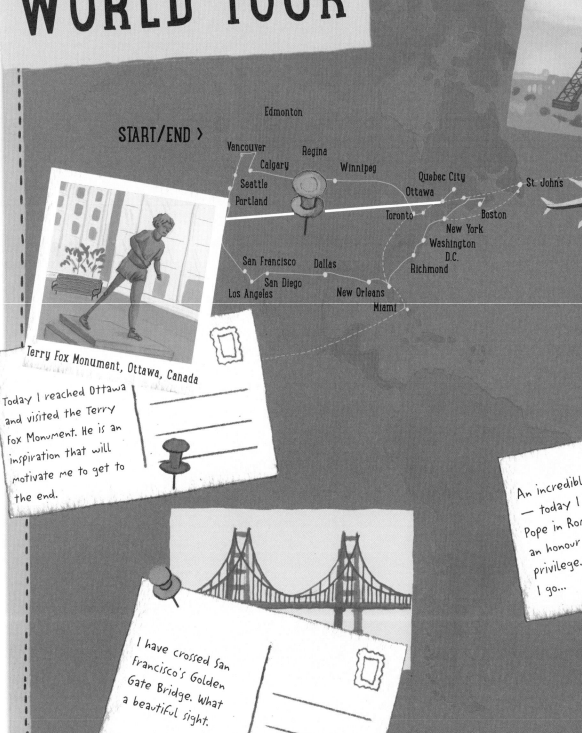

RICK HANSEN
MAN IN MOTION
WORLD TOUR

Paris

START/END >

Edmonton

Vancouver

Calgary

Regina

Winnipeg

Seattle

Portland

Quebec City

Ottawa

St. John's

Glasgow

Belfast

Dublin

Toronto

Boston

New York

Washington D.C.

Madrid

San Francisco

Dallas

Lisbon

Gibraltar

San Diego

Los Angeles

New Orleans

Richmond

Miami

Terry Fox Monument, Ottawa, Canada

Today I reached Ottawa and visited the Terry Fox Monument. He is an inspiration that will motivate me to get to the end.

I have crossed San Francisco's Golden Gate Bridge. What a beautiful sight.

An incredible moment — today I met the Pope in Rome. It was an honour and a privilege. Onwards I go...

Vatican City

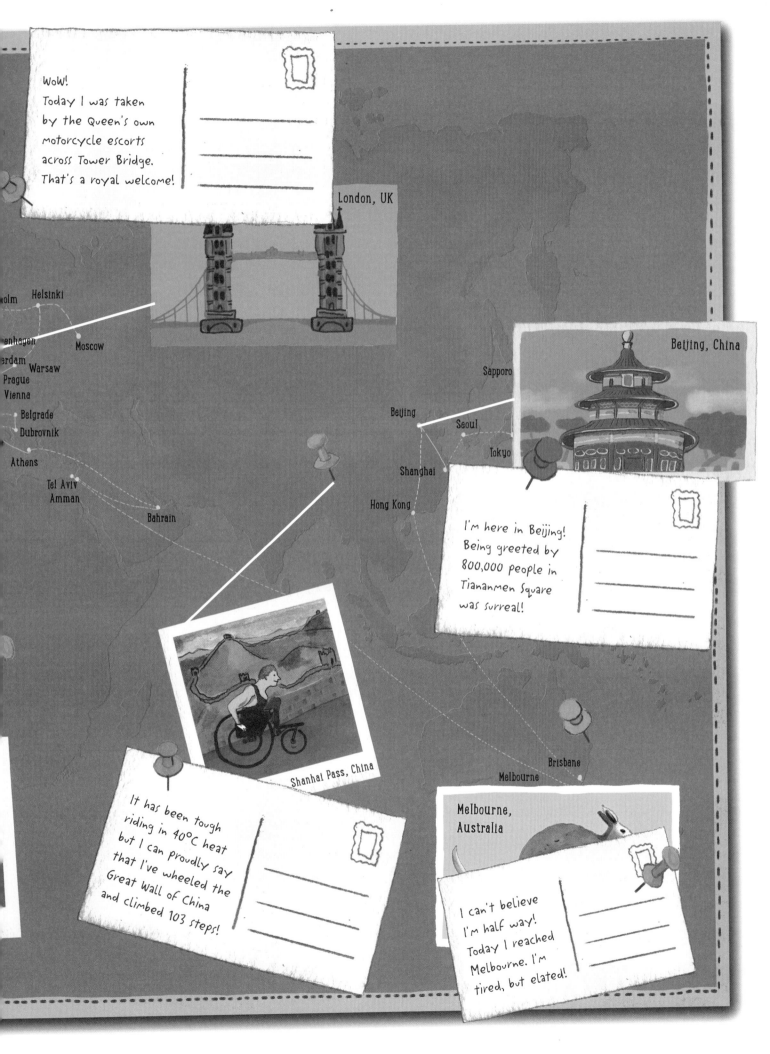

WoW!
Today I was taken by the Queen's own motorcycle escorts across Tower Bridge. That's a royal welcome!

London, UK

Helsinki
olm
enhagen
Moscow
rdam
Warsaw
Prague
Vienna
Belgrade
Dubrovnik
Athens
Tel Aviv
Amman
Bahrain

Sapporo

Beijing, China

Beijing
Seoul
Tokyo
Shanghai
Hong Kong

I'm here in Beijing! Being greeted by 800,000 people in Tiananmen Square was surreal!

Shanhai Pass, China

It has been tough riding in 40°C heat but I can proudly say that I've wheeled the Great Wall of China and climbed 103 steps!

Brisbane
Melbourne

Melbourne, Australia

I can't believe I'm half way! Today I reached Melbourne. I'm tired, but elated!

TOTAL NUMBER OF COUNTRIES VISITED: 34

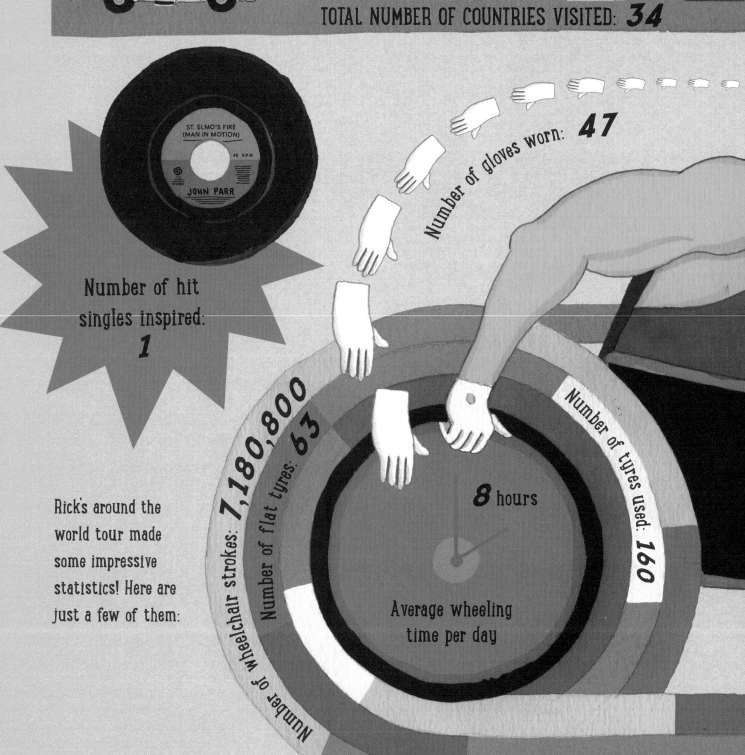

ST. ELMO'S FIRE
(MAN IN MOTION)

45 R.P.M

STEREO

JOHN PARR

Number of hit singles inspired: **1**

Number of gloves worn: **47**

Rick's around the world tour made some impressive statistics! Here are just a few of them:

Number of wheelchair strokes: **7,180,800**

Number of flat tyres: **63**

Number of tyres used: **160**

8 hours

Average wheeling time per day

NUMBER OF
LETTERS RECEIVED:
200,000

RICK HANSEN

Rick Hansen

GREETINGS from NEWFOUNDLAND

Postcards
written:
1,086

$26,000,000
in donations

DERVLA MURPHY

For half a century, Dervla Murphy has been travelling the world.
She has written more than 25 books about her adventures.
It all began on her tenth birthday, when Dervla's parents gave
her a second-hand bicycle and her grandfather sent her an atlas.
The world suddenly opened up before her. She began to dream
of pedalling all the way to India...

Twenty years later, Dervla put her dream into action, cycling all the way from Dunkirk in France to Delhi in India – a distance of nearly 8,000 km! Her first big adventure began during the coldest winter in memory. Dervla had to battle snowstorms and icy roads across Europe. But her problems didn't stop there. One freezing night in Bulgaria, Dervla even had to shoot snarling wolves when they surrounded her.

TRAVELLING SOLO

At the time, a woman travelling alone on a bicycle was a very unusual sight so huge crowds gathered to stare at Dervla everywhere she went.

These grew larger the further east she rode, heading through Turkey towards Afghanistan, then over the mighty Himalayan mountains to Pakistan and on to India.

DESCENDING INTO THE VALLEY

In Pakistan, Dervla spent a terrible day carrying and dragging her bike up a slippery, snow-covered mountain. Descending into the valley on the other side, she discovered that the bridge across the river had collapsed. Cold, exhausted and worried that she might have to return the way she had come, Dervla had to think on her feet. By pure chance, she managed to wrap her arm round the neck of a small cow that was about to cross the river, and together they waded across!

> **"** I set out to enjoy myself by seeing the world, not to make or break any record. **"**

KEEPING IT SIMPLE

Dervla liked to travel very simply. Her bicycle only had three gears but she had them removed because she felt they would be too sensitive to survive the rocky roads of Asia. Despite this, most days she still managed to cover more than 100 km!

Before leaving home she posted four spare tyres to various addresses on her route because most places did not have bike shops – a very smart idea! Dervla carried her gear in two small panniers, a saddle bag and a small rucksack. She carried her passport and money in a belt hidden round her waist.

KIT

1. reading books
2. diary and pencils
3. toothbrush
4. thermal underwear
5. woolen balaclava
6. spare inner tube
7. chlorine tablets (for water purification)
8. sun cream
9. loose shirt
10. puncture repair kit

Afghanistan

I'm here in Kabul! It's been a tough journey so far, but it has been worth it. It's so hot here I need to go and find myself a nice cold drink and some shade!

Tehran

India

I can't believe I'm here! My dream of cycling to India is complete. I'm feeling so proud and emotional. Now I can sit back and reflect on everything I've achieved. Time to start planning the next trip!

Turkey ✈ AIR MAIL

Here I am in Turkey! I'm now half way in my journey to India. It feels incredible to have reached this milestone. Cycling every day has been thirsty work, and I've built up quite an appetite! Luckily, I love Turkish food.

Why Dervla Murphy Inspired Me

Dervla Murphy is wonderfully normal. She doesn't claim to be an athlete, an 'adventurer', or anything other than she is — a straight-talking, kind woman. She implies that anyone could do the adventures she does. Just stop making excuses and get out there! Dervla is an important role model for girls, not least of all because she will probably hate this sentence, seeing no reason at all why girls shouldn't cycle across continents just like boys.

Full Tilt was one of the first cycling books I read when I began dreaming of travelling. My own first bicycle adventure was cycling through Pakistan into China.

RANULPH FIENNES

A prolific explorer, Sir Ranulph Fiennes has tackled polar journeys, crossed deserts, climbed Everest and discovered lost cities. His expeditions have raised millions for charity and even though he is more than 70 years old, his adventures continue today. *Guinness World Records* called Ranulph the 'World's Greatest Living Explorer' whilst Prince Charles described him as 'mad but marvellous'. One of Ranulph's biggest adventures – the Transglobe Expedition – took seven years of preparation, before they even reached the start line!

Ranulph has had a colourful life to say the least! After being thrown out of the SAS (Special Air Service) for blowing up a movie set that was spoiling a pretty English village, he began 50 years of tackling extreme expeditions. Ranulph is unusual amongst explorers for not specialising in one kind of adventure – from running to climbing, Ranulph has achieved extraordinary feats – and there's no sign of him stopping!

FROM CROCODILES TO PENGUINS

One of Ranulph's first journeys was to travel 6,400 km up the River Nile by hovercraft, from the Mediterranean Sea to the source of the world's longest river. The local people had never seen a hovercraft before Ranulph and his friends zoomed by!

But most of his journeys are human-powered. Ranulph spent 90 days crossing the Antarctic landmass on skis with a friend, each man pulling a sled with more than 200 kg of food and supplies – about the same as two fully-grown sheep!

REDISCOVERED RUINS

Ranulph's expeditions have even led to the rediscovery of the legendary lost city of Ubar. Thousands of years ago, Ubar was a wealthy city on Arabia's frankincense trading route. Over time it became buried in the sands of the Empty Quarter desert in Oman. Ranulph and a team of archaeologists used old texts and satellite images to narrow down their search and find the city again. They unearthed ruined towers, 250,000-year-old axe heads, and chess pieces more than a thousand years old.

" Pick your team on character, not skill. "

WORLD RUNNER

Ranulph once ran seven marathons in seven days on seven continents, despite having a heart attack just five months before! "I want to drink hot chocolate and eat chicken curry!" he declared at the end.

Ranulph completed the 250-km Marathon des Sables in the Sahara Desert, aged 71, struggling over the ferociously hot sand dunes. It's often called the 'Toughest Race on Earth'!

FACE YOUR FEARS

Although he has a fear of heights, Ranulph reached the summit of Mount Everest on his third attempt, aged 65. Do you think your grandad could climb Everest?

Sir Ranulph's latest goal is to become the first person to cross both polar ice caps and also to climb the highest peak on each continent, known as the Seven Summits.

Why Ranulph Fiennes Inspired Me

Ranulph's varied expeditions are all about determination and pushing your limits. He has lived a truly adventurous life but also helped others through his fundraising. *Living Dangerously* was the first adventure book I ever read. It became my inspiration and guide. For years I used Ranulph as a standard to measure myself against. Ranulph was my first adventure hero.

THE ARCTIC OCEAN

RANULPH FIENNES SET OUT TO WALK SOLO AND UNSUPPORTED (THAT MEANS NO OUTSIDE HELP OR SUPPLIES) TO THE NORTH POLE. AS THERE IS NO LAND, YOU MUST WALK ACROSS FROZEN SEA ICE AND SOMETIMES CROSS OPEN WATER – AND THERE'S ALWAYS THE RISK OF MEETING A HUNGRY POLAR BEAR...

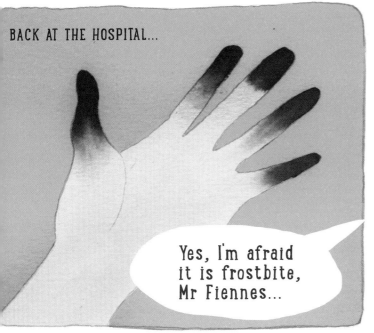

BACK AT THE HOSPITAL...

Yes, I'm afraid it is frostbite, Mr Fiennes...

...we will have to operate. But there is a waiting list.

HOSPITAL

These dead finger ends are so painful! I can't face having to wait months before the operation.

I have an idea!

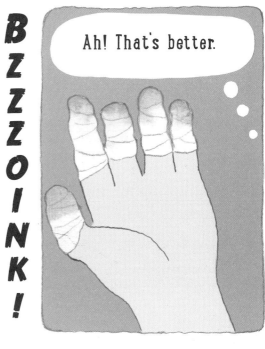

BZZZOINK!

Ah! That's better.

THE TRANSGLOBE EXPEDITION

The Transglobe Expedition was one of the most ambitious adventures ever attempted. Dreamed up by Ranulph's wife, Ginny, Ranulph told her that the expedition was impossible because it had never been done, to which Ginny called her husband 'pathetic'! Then the pair got to work and made the impossible possible. It took seven years to prepare for the trip and Ranulph and Ginny had to secure sponsors for every single item they planned to take – shoelaces included!

Taking three years to complete, the Transglobe Expedition was the first to ever make a circumpolar navigation, meaning the team went round the world via the North and South Poles, without leaving the Earth's surface. Through this expedition, Ginny became Britain's most experienced polar radio operator.

Here are some awesome facts about the trip:

6 MONTHS

The team built a base camp with huts made of cardboard. This kept them safe and sheltered through the long, dark winter months in Antarctica.

90 KILOGRAMS

The team trudged across the Arctic hauling sleds that weighed around 90 kg! That's about three times as heavy as a big dog.

ROAD ATLAS

1ST WOMAN

Ginny was the first woman to be awarded the Polar Medal after the expedition was complete.

1 YEAR

A crew of volunteeers were selected from around the world over an intensive year-long process.

1 PET DOG

Ranulph took his beloved dog Bothie on the trip – the first dog to have visited (and peed on) both poles! Bothie wore a specially designed suit and hat to keep him warm.

7 YEARS

The trip took seven years to plan.

99 DAYS

Ranulph and his teammate Charlie drifted across the Arctic Ocean for 99 days on an ice floe until the Benjamin Bowring expedition ship rescued them.

1,900 SPONSORS

1,900 sponsors were needed to cover the costs of the trip.

-40°C

Temperatures in the Arctic reached -40°C!

1) The team set sail from Greenwich on an icebreaker ship called the Benjamin Bowring.

2) Arriving in Africa, Ranulph and the crew drove across the Sahara desert in a four-wheel-drive truck.

3) They rejoined the ship in Côte d'Ivoire and sailed around the African coast.

4) The team arrived in Antarctica at the end of summer and set up camp to overwinter.

5) When spring returned, Ranulph and his crew crossed Antarctica on snowmobiles, via the South Pole.

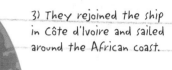

①

Vancouver
Los Angeles

N. AMERICA

Ellesmere Island • North Pole
• Spitzbergen

Greenwich
Barcelona • Paris EUROPE
② Algiers

③ Abidjan   AFRICA

Cape Town

6) After reaching the other side, Ranulph's team sailed north on the Benjamin Bowring.

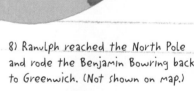

⑥

AUSTRALIA
Sydney   Auckland

⑤
McMurdo Sound
South Pole
ANTARCTICA
④ SANAE

7) Ranulph and his friend Charlie crossed the Arctic, by small boat and then on foot. (Not shown on map.)

8) Ranulph reached the North Pole and rode the Benjamin Bowring back to Greenwich. (Not shown on map.)

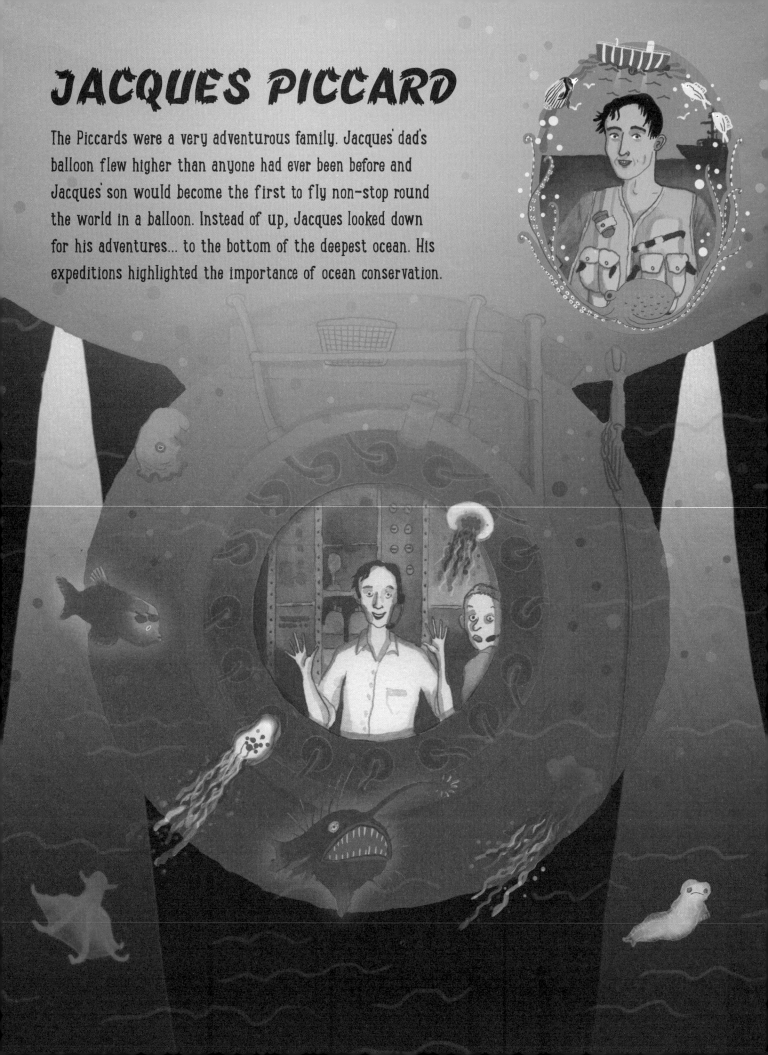

JACQUES PICCARD

The Piccards were a very adventurous family. Jacques' dad's balloon flew higher than anyone had ever been before and Jacques' son would become the first to fly non-stop round the world in a balloon. Instead of up, Jacques looked down for his adventures... to the bottom of the deepest ocean. His expeditions highlighted the importance of ocean conservation.

Trieste bathyscaphe

It is bitterly cold and permanently dark at the bottom of the ocean because sunlight can't reach it. As you travel deeper, the weight of the water above creates enormous pressure that would crush bodies or normal submarines. In some ways, the conditions are even harsher than those on the moon. These were the conditions that Jacques faced on his deep-sea mission. Do you think you could have endured it?

PREPARATIONS

Jacques and his dad built incredibly strong bathyscaphes (the name for submarines that can go very deep). Their first attempt reached nearly 1.5 km deep. When their second machine reached double the depth at 3 km, Jacques gave up his job to work full time on improving the bathyscaphe.

The final model, named Trieste, had two parts: a crew cabin and a float. Suspended beneath the float, the cabin had to resist nearly 150,000 tonnes of pressure. If it cracked, Jacques and his friend Don Walsh would be crushed instantly. Despite the dangers, the two men were willing to take the risk in order to explore where no man had ever been before.

GOING DOWN

At around 10,900 m, the Challenger Deep is the very deepest part of the Mariana Trench in the Pacific Ocean. To help them sink to the bottom, Jacques and Don carried nine tonnes of iron, which they would dump in order to float back up to the surface again. The descent to the Challenger Deep took almost five hours, dropping at a rate of 90 cm a second. At 9,000 m the cabin windows cracked, but the men continued their descent, determined to carry on.

ROCK BOTTOM

Upon finally reaching the bottom, a relieved Jacques and Don shook hands and opened a chocolate bar! The Trieste could not collect samples or take photographs, so they couldn't gather scientific data, but it was well worth the effort. No human had ever reached the depths of the ocean before. After spending only 20 minutes at the bottom, the pair began their three-hour ascent to the surface.

LESSONS LEARNED

The Trieste's main achievement was to prove that the journey was possible. They also discovered that some remarkable creatures were able to survive in those extreme conditions at the very deepest point of our planet. This discovery led to a ban on the dumping of nuclear waste at sea. After Jacques and Don returned to the surface, nobody else repeated the dive until the Deepsea Challenger, half a century later.

> " The best we can hope to do is to understand nature and obey it. "

Deepsea Challenger

THE MARIANA TRENCH

Jacques Piccard and Don Walsh were the first people to reach the bottom of the Mariana Trench in the North Pacific Ocean, more than 10,000 m underwater. This is the lowest point on the surface of Earth's crust. Here's an infographic that visualises just how deep this really is.

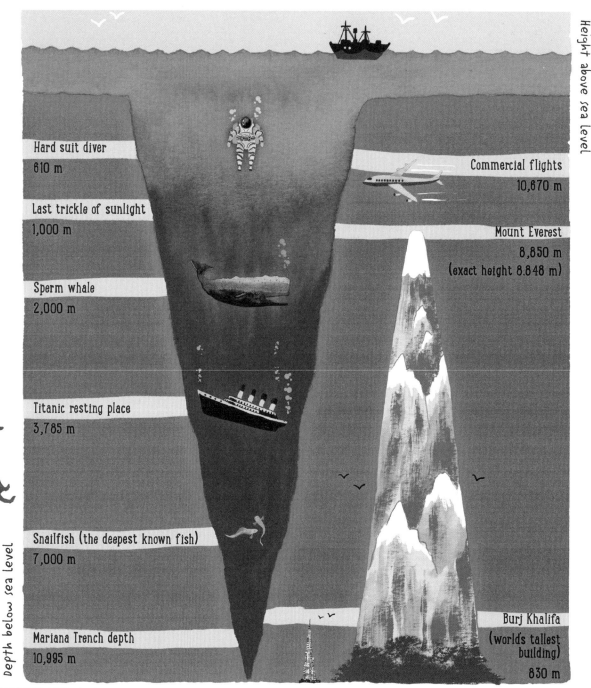

Height above sea level

Depth below sea level

Hard suit diver
610 m

Last trickle of sunlight
1,000 m

Sperm whale
2,000 m

Titanic resting place
3,785 m

Snailfish (the deepest known fish)
7,000 m

Mariana Trench depth
10,995 m

Commercial flights
10,670 m

Mount Everest
8,850 m
(exact height 8,848 m)

Burj Khalifa
(world's tallest building)
830 m

Why Jacques Piccard Inspired Me

Jacques Piccard's adventures happened at a similar time to the moon landings. Both projects involved inhospitable places and would have been unimaginable even ten years earlier without extraordinary advances in technology. Hundreds of people have travelled into space, and 12 have walked on the moon, but only three people are part of Jacques' exclusive club. I admire how much he cared about protecting the planet and am fascinated by people willing to put themselves in situations in which no one knows what will happen. We need humans who are curious, intelligent and brave.

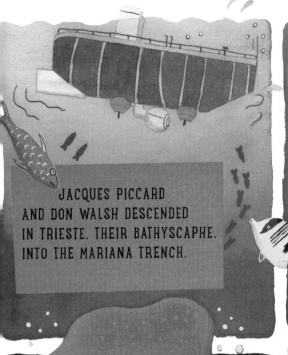

JACQUES PICCARD AND DON WALSH DESCENDED IN TRIESTE, THEIR BATHYSCAPHE, INTO THE MARIANA TRENCH.

THEY DIVED DEEPER AND DEEPER...

...BUT AT 9,000 METRES...

CRACK!

THEY FEARED THE WORST.

TURNING OFF THE EQUIPMENT, THEY LISTENED IN SILENCE, WAITING AND HOPING...

OK, let's continue!

THE TRIESTE LANDED SOFTLY AT THE TRENCH BOTTOM.

WHOOSH!

THE MEN CELEBRATED WITH CHOCOLATE...

...AND RECEIVED A PLEASANT SURPRISE.

OUI, ALLO! I CAN HEAR YOU ON THE HYDROPHONIC SYSTEM!

A DEEP-SEA PHONE CALL!

MICHAEL COLLINS

Whilst Neil Armstrong and Buzz Aldrin took their one small step onto the moon and into fame, astronaut Michael Collins' vital job was to fly the main spacecraft round and round the moon until it was time to collect the other two and return to Earth. When he was round the back of the moon and out of radio contact, Michael was the most isolated human that had ever lived.

As pilot of the command module, called Columbia, Michael was left all alone whilst his two friends became the first to walk on the moon. They landed in a module called Eagle, but Michael remained in orbit. Each time he flew around the back of the moon, Michael lost radio contact with Earth. But Michael loved the excitement and the importance of the mission and never felt lonely. If anything had gone wrong with Eagle, Neil and Buzz would have had to be abandoned on the moon, so Michael was very relieved when his friends returned to him successfully.

Hello?

ASTRONAUT TRAINING

On a journey into space, one tiny mistake can quickly lead to disaster. Preparing for adventures often requires far more time and effort than the trip itself – and being an astronaut requires more skill than any other kind of adventure! That was certainly true for Michael, Neil and Buzz as they prepared for the first ever journey to the moon. The training was incredibly tough and careful planning was needed.

FROM ROCKET SCIENCE TO SPACE ROCKS

Firstly, to be an astronaut, you need to understand a lot of maths and science. Michael said that the most important equipment for an astronaut is a ruler and pencil, which doesn't sound very adventurous! The next stage of training involved hundreds of hours of flying skills, learning to navigate from the stars and studying geology so that they could research Moon rocks. But of all the training the astronauts went through, the centrifuge training was the worst. It involved being spun round and round until they felt sick! This prepared the astronauts for the G-forces they faced when their spacecraft rushed back into Earth's atmosphere.

WE HAVE LIFT OFF

After basic training, each astronaut became an expert in particular skills. No one could learn everything, but as a team, Michael, Neil and Buzz had all the knowledge needed to attempt something that had never been done.

Michael felt lucky to be involved in such a famous adventure, though he did feel pressure because he knew that the whole world was watching. On top of that, the journey to the moon and back was dangerous as well as difficult. Blasting off in Apollo 11 must have been nerve-wracking, but to be able to say that he was part of such an historic expedition was worth all the hard work and worry.

" I know that I would be a liar or a fool if I said that I have the best of the three Apollo 11 seats, but I can say with truth that I am perfectly satisfied with the one I have. "

KIT

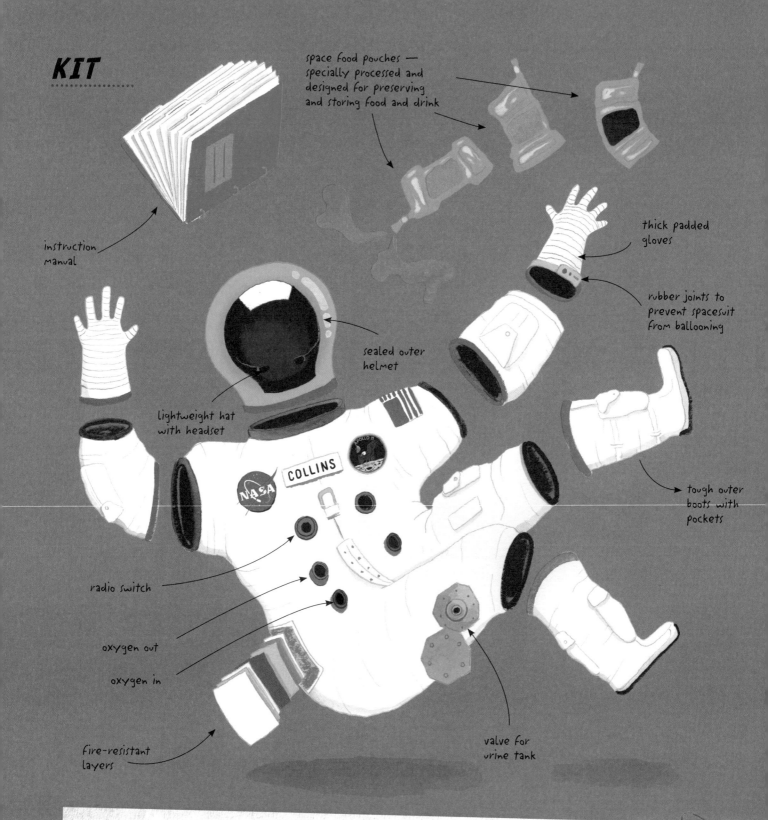

space food pouches — specially processed and designed for preserving and storing food and drink

instruction manual

thick padded gloves

rubber joints to prevent spacesuit from ballooning

sealed outer helmet

lightweight hat with headset

tough outer boots with pockets

COLLINS

NASA

radio switch

oxygen out

oxygen in

valve for urine tank

fire-resistant layers

Why Michael Collins Inspired Me

I admire people whose actions speak louder than their words. Michael Collins was part of the team that completed the greatest adventure in history. Without him, it would not have succeeded. Yet most people today do not even know his name. Michael would have loved to walk on the moon but that was not his role. I like how he acknowledged this but was also grateful for the amazing things he *did* get to do.

DEAR DIARY

Well, it's not long now until we head for the moon. What a wild thing to write! A lot of hard work, a bit of a brain, and a dollop of luck got me into this adventure. It's Sunday, my one day of the week to relax. I've just cooked a delicious lamb curry (I made a mess of the kitchen, though!) and enjoyed playing with my dog, Dubhe. Everything seems so normal.

BANG My poor wife, Patricia, seems worried. I understand that. We're going to be flying at 40, 500 km/s — that's pretty fast! I guess I'm a bit uneasy too, especially about the launch when something

is most likely to go wrong. There's so much fuel in our rocket that an explosion would be like sitting on 2,000 tonnes of TNT. I prefer not to think about that! I don't want to make any silly mistakes and embarrass myself either. But mostly I am excited about the adventure!

Helicopter training yesterday was great fun, and taught us a lot about flying a spacecraft. It's like rubbing your tummy and patting your head at the same time. It was better than learning about rocks, which we have been dragged all over the world to do. We also had to learn jungle and desert survival skills in case we don't land back on Earth exactly where we're supposed to.

My adventure is going to have a big impact on Patricia and our lovely three kids. No one thinks much about the loved ones that adventurers leave behind when we head off chasing our crazy dreams. But it's scary and lonely for them. Ann and Michael are only four and three, so don't really understand. But Kate's seven and she understands what I'm going to try to do. I'm glad she likes the idea of Daddy being an astronaut and doesn't seem too worried about it. I'll miss them all when I'm up there!

Mike

ROBYN DAVIDSON

Robyn Davidson knew nothing about camels, deserts or expeditions. She only knew she wanted an adventure in the Australian Outback. Robyn moved to Alice Springs and spent two years learning how to handle camels and survive in the desert. Only then did she feel prepared to begin her trek across the desert.

Two years after arriving in Alice Springs with just a suitcase of unsuitable clothes, $6 and her dog, Robyn was ready to set out on an incredible journey across the desert. Camels have a ferocious bite and kick, so learning how to handle them was hard work. She also had to overcome many doubters who did not believe she would survive.

Bone dry and unimaginably vast, the Australian Outback is a daunting place for an inexperienced traveller, but it is also beautiful with breathtaking landscapes and wildlife such as kangaroos and cockatoos. Robyn took more than six months to cover the 2,700 km to the ocean. The adventure pushed her to her mental and physical limits.

LONG DAYS

Robyn mostly travelled with only her four camels (Dookie, Bub, Zeleika and her calf Goliath) and her beloved dog, Diggity, for company. Each morning, Robyn woke early, boiled tea, packed the gear and saddled the camels. At night, the camels roamed to search for food so Robyn had to find them in the morning by following the sound of their bells. One of her most frightening experiences was the day she thought they had all run away. Without the camels, Robyn would certainly have died before reaching safety. What would you have done in that situation?

> " The two important things that I did learn were that you are as strong as you allow yourself to be, and that the most difficult part of any endeavour is taking the first step. "

NEW FRIEND

One night Robyn dreamed that an old Aboriginal man befriended her and helped with her adventure. Later on the journey, when she was feeling lonely, a Pitjantjatjara man called Mr Eddie appeared from nowhere. He travelled with Robyn for the next 300 km. Mr Eddie could not speak English but he and Robyn communicated by miming and acting, laughing happily at each other.

A WONDERFUL SIGHT

When Robyn eventually reached the Pacific Ocean, after six long, hard months, her camels were very confused. They had never seen so much water before and were disappointed that they could not drink the salty water. But Robyn managed to persuade her beloved animals to wade into the sea so that they could all celebrate together. I bet that felt amazing after trekking in the scorching heat!

The map shows a route across Australia:

START — Glen Helen tourist camp — Areyonga — Uluru (Ayres Rock) at Mutitjulu — Carnegie — Glenayle — Wiluna — Gibson Desert — Great Victoria Desert — FINISH Hamelin Pool

KIT

1. barrels of water
2. sleeping mat
3. shackles (for hobbling the camels at night)
4. food
5. dog food
6. swag (a portable bedroll)
7. rope
8. compass
9. change of clothes
10. sheepskin rug
11. muzzle for camels
12. blanket
13. map

ROBYN'S GOLDEN RULE

Robyn's golden rule when camping was to always care for the camels before herself. They were the most important part of the adventure. After a long day, Robyn removed their loads and saddles, then hobbled them so that they could search for food without straying too far. Only after she had done that would she build a camp fire and cook her own dinner (usually a tin of stew). Finally, she climbed into her sleeping bag, called a swag, and fell asleep. She often slept beside the fire because the desert nights were cold – temperatures could drop to less than 5°C.

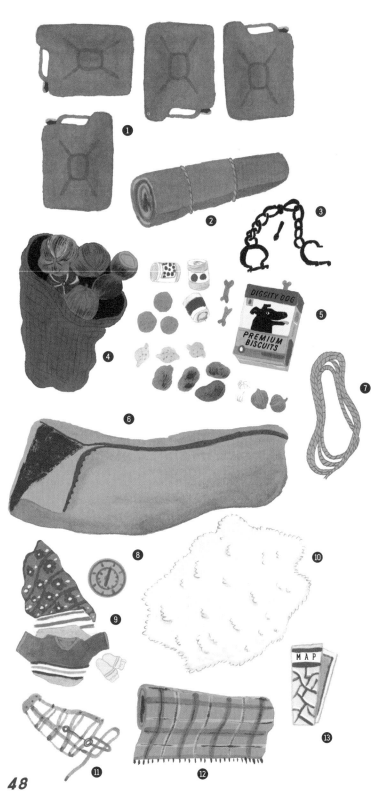

Why Robyn Davidson Inspired Me

Robyn knew nothing about camels or expeditions but she did not let that stop her. It would have been easier to say "people like me don't go on adventures like this," but Robyn persevered until she was almost competent enough to begin. The rest she learned along the way. I have always wanted an adventure in the Outback. Robyn's brilliant book, *Tracks*, with its beautiful photography. adds to that dream.

49

FELICE BENUZZI

During World War II, Italian Felice Benuzzi was captured in Kenya. He was placed in a prisoner-of-war camp overlooking the peaks of Mount Kenya. The boredom of prison life, combined with the tantalising view of the mountain, made Felice yearn for freedom and adventure. Although it's not easy for someone locked in prison to climb a mountain, Felice dared to dream big!

Both climbing a 5,000-m mountain and escaping from a prisoner-of-war camp are risky undertakings. Although seemingly impossible, that is exactly what Felice dreamed of doing!

Felice found two friends willing to join his adventure and others who would help their secret preparations. It took imagination and cunning to make ice axes, crampons and other equipment from items they could find or steal in the prison without getting caught by the guards. The preparations took eight months. Felice planned their route from the only map they had: a drawing of Mount Kenya on a tin of Oxo cubes! Before they could even set foot on the mountain, they first had to escape from their prison camp. Then they had to climb a very difficult mountain. Finally, they planned to then break *back into* the prison camp!

The inmates were on such slim rations that they were only able to collect a few spare raisins here and there as extra food on the trip. Do you think they would fill you up after a huge mountain climb?

> " The more I considered the idea of escape, the more I realised the magnitude of the task I had set myself. "

Why Felice Benuzzi Inspired Me

I love the joy of this adventure: hatching plans with your friends, the beauty of Africa and the challenge of attempting something difficult in the mountains. It was made all the more complicated by being a prisoner!

Felice's determination that even war and prison would not stop his dreams is inspiring. It reminds us that if you are determined enough, then you can make adventures happen.

KIT THEY HAD

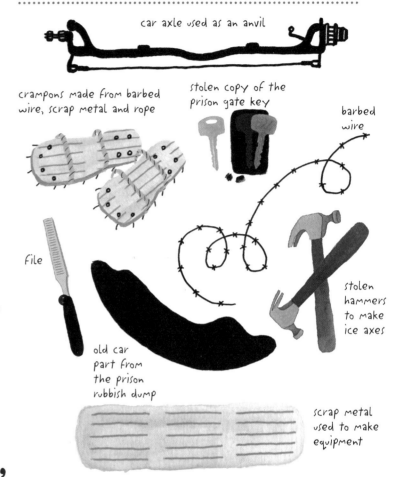

car axle used as an anvil

crampons made from barbed wire, scrap metal and rope

stolen copy of the prison gate key

barbed wire

File

old car part from the prison rubbish dump

stolen hammers to make ice axes

scrap metal used to make equipment

KIT THEY SHOULD HAVE HAD!

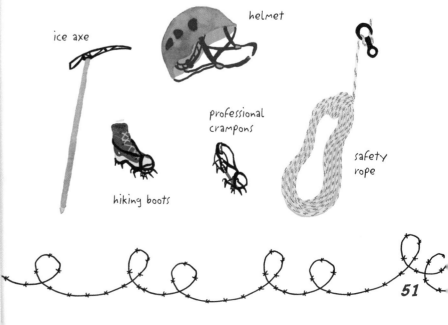

ice axe

helmet

professional crampons

hiking boots

safety rope

WHEN MOUNT KENYA CALLED, THEY NEEDED...

RUBBISH RAIDS!

SECRET DEALS!

The Great

ESCAPE PLAN

STARRING...
Felice Benuzzi
Vincenzo Barsotti
Giovanni Balletto

STOLEN EQUIPMENT!

KIT HIDDEN IN THE TOMATOES!

I'm too tired to carry on. I'll meet you later!

We made it! Just look at that view.

Felice! Giovanni! You made it back alive!

This will be a feast!

Plain rice has never tasted so good!

Excuse me, Colonel, we have a small confession to make...

You CLIMBED MOUNT KENYA? Well done, men! But wait – you must be punished for escaping.

Ah. Just one more day stuck in this cell...

Yes, but it was all the better for it in the long run.

SARAH OUTEN

Sarah Outen spent four years rowing, cycling and kayaking round the world. She was hit by a tropical storm on the Pacific Ocean and a hurricane whilst crossing the Atlantic. The journey definitely did not go to plan, but Sarah says that it was all the better for that in the long run.

Can you imagine taking a four-and-a-half-year journey around the world via land and sea? Well, that's exactly what Sarah Outen did! After months of training, Sarah began her adventure by paddling out of London, UK, and across the English Channel, arriving in France nine hours later. She then jumped on her bicycle, Hercules, and rode east, covering more than 16,000 km across Europe, Central Asia and China. The journey was both gruelling and exhilarating, and Sarah learnt a lot on the way about herself and the kindness of people she met.

HURRICANES AND STORMS

The biggest challenge Sarah faced was rowing across the oceans solo (although she rowed her first ocean when she was just 24). She capsized 20 times, was rescued after a tropical storm on the Pacific Ocean damaged her boat, and was also picked up on the Atlantic Ocean before a hurricane struck. For most people, these experiences would be enough to make them never return to the sea again, but Sarah found the motivation to continue her journey. It is a good reminder that adventurers must have perseverance, be positive and always be willing to try again. It is also a reminder of how fierce the natural world can be, and shows the risks that people are willing to take in pursuit of their adventurous dreams.

SHARING THE ADVENTURE

Amidst the drama, Sarah's adventure was filled with plenty of wonderful moments, too. Whilst in China, Sarah met a young man called Gao who was fascinated by her adventure – he had never known it was possible to cycle across a whole country. Gao decided to cycle to Beijing with Sarah and bought a bike the very next day. Together they cycled 4,800 km across China. His spirit of adventure

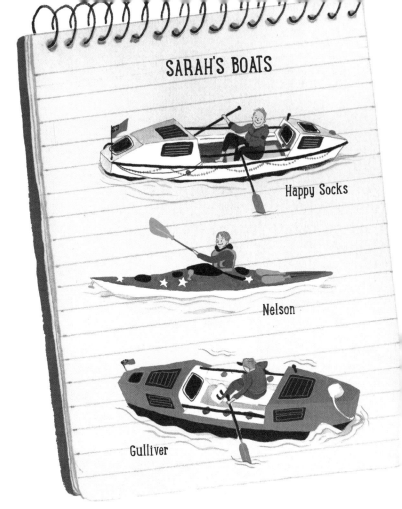

SARAH'S BOATS

Happy Socks

Nelson

Gulliver

was exactly what Sarah had hoped to inspire in people through her journey, and it might do the same for you, too.

END OF THE WORLD

Touching land back in the UK at long last, Sarah was joined by friends and family as she cycled the final stretch. Her adventure finished by paddling under Tower Bridge in London, completing her 40,000 km journey. Despite all the challenges, Sarah had made it around the world!

> " What's stopping you? It's you, isn't it? "

Why Sarah Outen Inspired Me

Kayaking at sea is challenging. Ocean rowing requires many different skills and can be extremely dangerous. Cycling across a continent is tough. Sarah combined all these in her unique, fascinating journey. Traditionally, adventures have mostly been completed by men, but more women like Sarah are tackling epic challenges. She is a brilliant role model for girls dreaming of adventure.

START

SETTING OFF
Sarah took off from London, UK, kayaking across the English Channel towards France.

PEDALLING EAST
From France, Sarah cycled to China on her bicycle, Hercules. Whilst there, she was joined by young man for over 4,800 km.

NORTH PACIFIC ROW
Sarah left Japan once more, in her new boat, Happy Socks. Four months in, after many weeks of stormy weather, she changed course for Alaska.

RECOVERY & REBUILDING
She returned to the UK to recover before returning to Japan.

ALASKA
Justine joined Sarah once more, and they paddled together from Adak Island to Homer.

THE FINISH LINE
Sarah kayaked down the River Thames and back under Tower Bridge to complete her four-and-a-half-year, 40,000-km expedition.

FINISH

58

CROSSING TO JAPAN
Sarah kayaked over to Japan accompanied by her friend, Justine Curgenven.

PACIFIC ROW
Sarah started her solo row to Canada aboard Gulliver. But she was hit by a tropical storm and had to be rescued.

NORTH AMERICA
Sarah cycled across North America through one of the worst winters on record, from the Pacific to the Atlantic.

ATLANTIC ROW
She rowed across the North Atlantic Ocean, but a hurricane meant she was forced to abandon Happy Socks at sea.

THE UK HOME STRETCH
Sarah cycled from Falmouth to Oxford, UK, with friends, family and supporters.

IBN BATTUTA

Abu Abdallah Muhammad Ibn Battuta (known affectionately as 'Ibn', meaning 'son' in Arabic) was one of the most prolific travellers of all time, trekking further and for longer than even the legendary Marco Polo. He set off from Morocco on a donkey, aged 21, and did not come home for 30 years! Ibn Battuta travelled through much of the known world, crisscrossing Asia, the Middle East and Africa, seeing things that would have seemed unbelievable 700 years ago.

Ibn Battuta set off to visit Mecca (a holy city in Saudi Arabia that Muslims try to visit in their lifetime). Along the way, he realised that there were so many fascinating places in the world to explore. He wrote that he was sad to leave his parents but had a strong desire to visit more new countries.

> **I set out alone, having neither fellow traveller in whose companionship I might find cheer, nor caravan whose party I might join, but swayed by an impulse within me and a desire long-cherished in my bosom to visit these illustrious sanctuaries. So I braced my resolution to quit all my dear ones, and forsook my home as birds forsake their nests.**

MARVELS AND MAGIC
With no plan and only his curiosity to drive him onwards, a map of Ibn Battuta's adventures looks more like a spider's web than a route! He met fire-eaters, magicians and whirling dervishes. He even got married ten times along the way! Can you imagine what it must have felt like to meet these weird and wonderful people?

THE WORLD AT HIS FEET
As he travelled east, his horizons began to open. In Alexandria, Egypt, Ibn Battuta dreamed of flying on the wings of a huge bird to Yemen, and then east and south, 'alighting in some dark and greenish country'. After performing the pilgrimage to Mecca no fewer than five times, exploring Iraq, Iran and the

Persian Gulf, descending as far as what is now Kenya and living for a while in the Christian capital of Constantinople (once the largest and wealthiest city in Europe, Ibn Battuta passed through Crimea, Central Asia and Afghanistan to the state of Delhi in India.

A spiritual backpacker, Ibn Battuta braved thieves, blisters and his own prejudices. His journeys included trips to North Africa, the Horn of Africa, West Africa and Eastern Europe, as well as to the Middle East, South Asia, Central Asia, Southeast Asia and China. The sheer scope of his adventures was breathtaking. You could definitely argue that Ibn Battuta was the greatest traveller of all time.

In the mountains of Afghanistan, Ibn Battuta spread felt clothes in front of the camels for them to tread on, so they wouldn't sink in the snow.

Why Ibn Battuta Inspired Me

The scale of Ibn Battuta's travels was extraordinary. When I first dreamed of adventure, it was relatively easy to plan because I had already read stories and seen pictures of the wonders of the world. I knew that big journeys were possible because my heroes had done them before me. Ibn Battuta knew nothing at all when he set off. He was driven only by one thing – curiosity. That is perhaps an adventurer's most important characteristic.

THE TRAVELS OF IBN BATTUTA

This map shows just how much Ibn Battuta travelled during his 30-year adventure. The book about his journey is brilliantly called *A Gift to Those Who Contemplate the Wonders of Cities and the Marvels of Travelling* and some of the experiences he wrote about are shared here:

❾ He visited Adam's Peak in Sri Lanka (a sacred landmark said to contain the footprint of a sacred deity).

❽ He sailed as an ambassador from India to China on a ship laden with diplomatic gifts of silver and gold – until a storm sank the ship. Ibn washed up on a beach with nothing except a prayer carpet!

❼ Ibn Battuta spent eight years in Delhi, working as a judge.

His original goal for ⟨tra⟩velling, Ibn Battuta ⟨jou⟩rneyed to Mecca as part ⟨of⟩ a Muslim pilgrimage.

2 Ibn Battuta visited the Pharos Lighthouse of Alexandria twice. It was once one of the seven wonders of the world.

3 Near Alexandria, Ibn Battuta visited a saint. Whilst there, he had a dream that a large bird carried him far eastward. The saint told Ibn Battuta that this was a sign he would travel to India, which he later did.

The Travels of Ibn Battuta

Bukhara
Samarkand
Hindu Kush Mountains
Kabul
5
Multan
7 Delhi
⟨Ho⟩rmuz
INDIA
Muscat
Cambay
Daulatabad
6
Calicut
8
Chittagong
9
Adam's Peak, Sri Lanka
Maldives
Samudera
CHINA
Hanghou
Guangzhou
Quanzhou
Qui Nhon

6 On his way to the coast, Ibn Battuta ⟨a⟩nd his convoy were attacked by a group of ⟨b⟩andits. Despite being robbed and injured, ⟨h⟩e was able to safely make it to Delhi.

5 Ibn Battuta crossed the Khawak Pass in Afghanistan at a jaw-dropping 4,000 m high!

4 Ibn Battuta just missed the bubonic plague outbreak that was sweeping through Aleppo.

LAKPA RITA SHERPA

At just 21 years old, Lakpa Rita Sherpa made his first ascent of Mount Everest, the world's highest mountain. He has now climbed it an incredible 17 times! Lakpa is also the first Nepali to climb the highest peak on each continent, known as the Seven Summits.

The Sherpa people of Nepal have always been an essential support for Himalayan climbing expeditions. Life in the Himalayas can be tough. Sherpas live higher than any other community, nestled between steep valleys, snow-covered peaks and icy rivers. They are strong people, accustomed to working hard in difficult, high-altitude conditions.

HIGH HOPES

Inspired by fellow Sherpa mountaineer Tenzing Norgay, Lakpa became a climbing guide. Tenzing and Edmund Hillary were the first people to climb the world's highest mountain. To this day, Tenzing remains Lakpa's hero. After studying English at school, he dreamed of climbing Everest, and his uncle hired him to help out at Everest Base Camp. Since then, Lakpa has been on almost 30 expeditions to Mount Everest and is one of the few Sherpas working as a full-time mountain guide all around the world.

When you get hit by an avalanche, Lakpa advises 'you've got to swim, swim through the snow so you don't drown'.

DID YOU KNOW?

Many Sherpas are named after the day of the week they were born on. Lakpa was born on a Wednesday!

MONDAY: DAWA
TUESDAY: MIGMAR
WEDNESDAY: LAKPA
THURSDAY: PHURBA
FRIDAY: PASANG
SATURDAY: PEMBA
SUNDAY: NGIMA

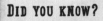

HUGE ACHIEVEMENTS

Lakpa's first expedition is one of his happiest memories of being on Mount Everest. He smiled every day, even though he was hit by an avalanche whilst ferrying cargo up the mountain! Lakpa didn't reach the summit that year, but he was learning fast. Simply staying alive in the mountains requires courage and skill.

REACHING THE SUMMIT

The first time Lakpa reached the highest point on Earth was when he guided a couple from Yugoslavia. At 21 years old, it was his biggest goal. As well as the pride of his achievement, Lakpa knew that successfully reaching the top meant an increase in his earning potential as a guide. He remembers it was a beautiful day – calm and sunny, without a breath of wind. Lakpa and the couple were able to spend 30 wonderful minutes on top of the world, soaking in the triumph and the glorious views. He could never have known then that he would return to those special few square metres another 16 times.

THAME, NEPAL

Lakpa grew up in a small, remote village and had six sisters and two brothers.

Every morning, just as the sun rose, nine-year-old Lakpa set off to school — a four-hour walk away...

...and a four-hour walk home in the dark, too!

One day, some special visitors arrived at Lakpa's school. It was his heroes, Tenzing Norgay and Edmund Hillary!

Lakpa listened carefully to the first people to reach the top of the world's highest mountain. He began dreaming of doing the same.

Feeling inspired, Lakpa worked hard to learn English - he knew he'd need to speak it to become a mountain guide.

It paid off! Lakpa's uncle gave him his first job - helping at Everest base camp.

Lakpa finished school and completed his first expedition. From then on, the only way was up!

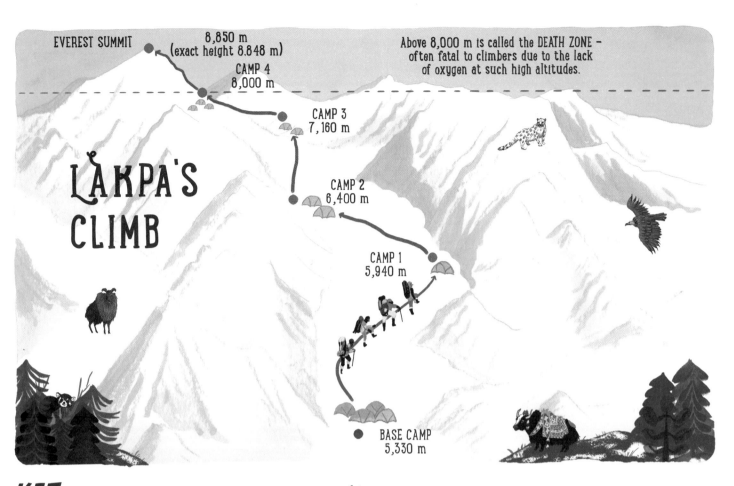

EVEREST SUMMIT — 8,850 m (exact height 8.848 m)

CAMP 4
8,000 m

Above 8,000 m is called the DEATH ZONE – often fatal to climbers due to the lack of oxygen at such high altitudes.

CAMP 3
7,160 m

LAKPA'S CLIMB

CAMP 2
6,400 m

CAMP 1
5,940 m

BASE CAMP
5,330 m

KIT

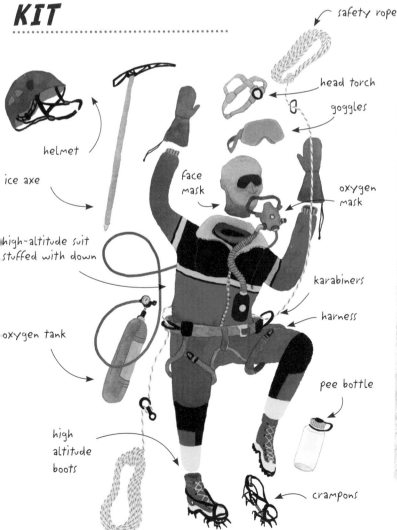

safety rope

head torch

goggles

helmet

ice axe

face mask

oxygen mask

high-altitude suit stuffed with down

karabiners

harness

oxygen tank

pee bottle

high altitude boots

crampons

Why Lakpa Rita Sherpa Inspired Me

The Everest books we read are often written by Westerners, who sometimes neglect the importance of the local Nepali climbers who make the expeditions possible. I wanted to highlight a culture that has helped every successful Everest expedition.

Lakpa has not only accomplished an astonishing list of mountaineering achievements, he has also helped many people along the way, saving some climbers' lives and guiding others to the summit. He is a fine role model to anyone dreaming of adventure.

NELLIE BLY

Elizabeth Jane Cochran is more familiarly known by her pen name, Nellie Bly. She was inspired by the popular book *Around the World in Eighty Days*, a fictional story about an attempt to race around the globe by a man named Phileas Fogg. Nellie, a journalist, wanted to see for herself whether it was possible to travel around the planet in such a short time. Not only did she succeed in completing the 36,400-km journey, she also smashed the 80 day record!

After reading *Around the World in Eighty Days*, Nellie Bly approached the newspaper where she worked with the idea of trying to match the adventure for real. She would try to race around the world faster than anyone had travelled before, sending back exciting stories along the way.

Her boss liked the idea, but said that only a man could accomplish something so difficult! Luckily, he changed his mind. He asked Nellie, "Can you start your trip round the world the day after tomorrow?" She answered, "I can start this minute!"

" If you want to do it, you can do it. The question is, do you want to do it? "

TRAVELLING LIGHT

The newspaper gave Nellie £200 in gold and banknotes (worth about £23,000 in today's money) to fund the trip. She carried the gold in her pocket, and the money in a bag round her neck whilst on the move.

Nellie travelled with only one small bag. She packed a few changes of underwear, but only one dress, made specially for her journey out of plain blue wool. Into her bag, Nellie managed to squeeze a dressing gown and tennis blazer, a pair of slippers, two caps, three veils and some handkerchiefs. She also carried a cup, a flask, needle and thread and writing materials. There was even space for a small jar of face cream – her one luxury item.

SETTING SAIL

Nellie set sail from New Jersey, USA. The clock started and the race began. She was very seasick at first, but soon recovered as the ship sailed across the Atlantic Ocean. Unbeknown to Nellie, at exactly the same time another newspaper sent a competitor round the world in the opposite direction. This meant that Nellie was now racing not only the clock, but also a rival, Elizabeth Bisland!

However, there was one detour that Nellie just couldn't resist – even when it threatened her very tight schedule. Jules Verne, the author of *Around the World in Eighty Days*, heard about Nellie's adventure and invited her to visit him in France. She accepted the invitation even though it meant racing to catch trains and a sleepless night or two.

In the end, Nellie arrived back in New Jersey in just 72 days, beating Phileas Fogg's time and Elizabeth too. Huge crowds gathered to welcome her home. No one in history had ever travelled round the world at such speed before!

KIT

① pen and ink
② needle and thread
③ handkerchiefs
④ slippers
⑤ change of underwear
⑥ bag
⑦ cap
⑧ flask
⑨ toothpaste
⑩ face cream

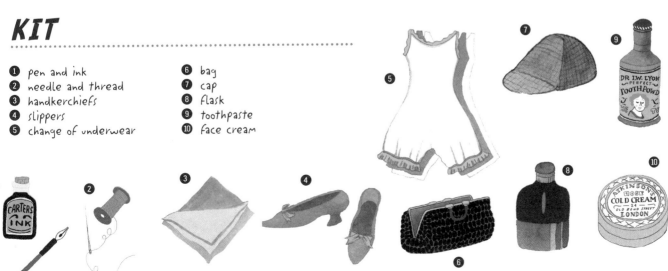

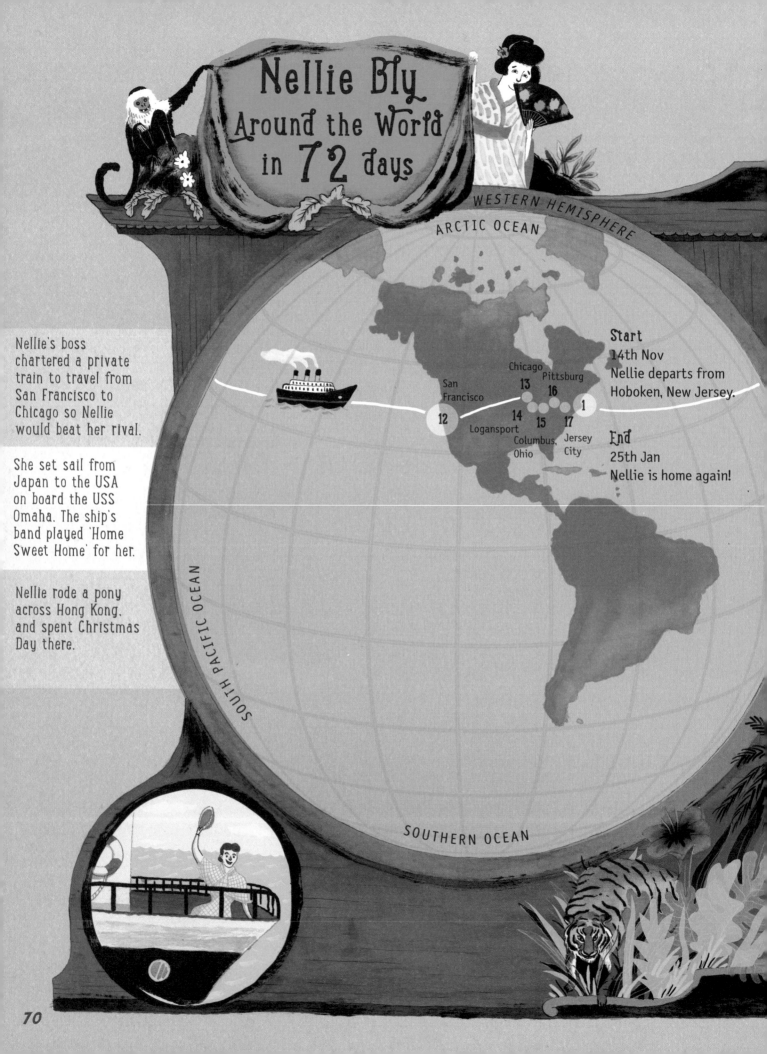

Nellie Bly
Around the World in 72 days

WESTERN HEMISPHERE

ARCTIC OCEAN

Nellie's boss chartered a private train to travel from San Francisco to Chicago so Nellie would beat her rival.

She set sail from Japan to the USA on board the USS Omaha. The ship's band played 'Home Sweet Home' for her.

Nellie rode a pony across Hong Kong, and spent Christmas Day there.

San Francisco

Chicago
13

Pittsburg
16

12

Logansport
14

Columbus, Ohio
15

17

1

Jersey City

Start
14th Nov
Nellie departs from Hoboken, New Jersey.

End
25th Jan
Nellie is home again!

SOUTH PACIFIC OCEAN

SOUTHERN OCEAN

Circling the globe at high speed in 1889 was both an endurance sport and a high-stakes puzzle. It meant sleepless nights, hurried connections and mad dashes to meet steamers in the rain – along with incredible memories! Here are a few of them:

EASTERN HEMISPHERE

ARCTIC OCEAN

NORTH PACIFIC OCEAN

2 London, England

3 Amiens, France

4 Brindisi, Italy

5 Port Said, Egypt

Aden, Yemen **6**

Colombo, Sri Lanka

7

Penang, Malaysia

8

9

Singapore

10 Hong Kong

11 Yokohama, Japan

INDIAN OCEAN

SOUTHERN OCEAN

In Egypt, Nellie watched a group of men catch a crocodile on the beach, by pinning it down and tying it with a rope.

Whilst in Singapore, Nellie bought a monkey.

She fell in love with Japan. Nellie wrote in her diary that it 'delighted the finer senses'.

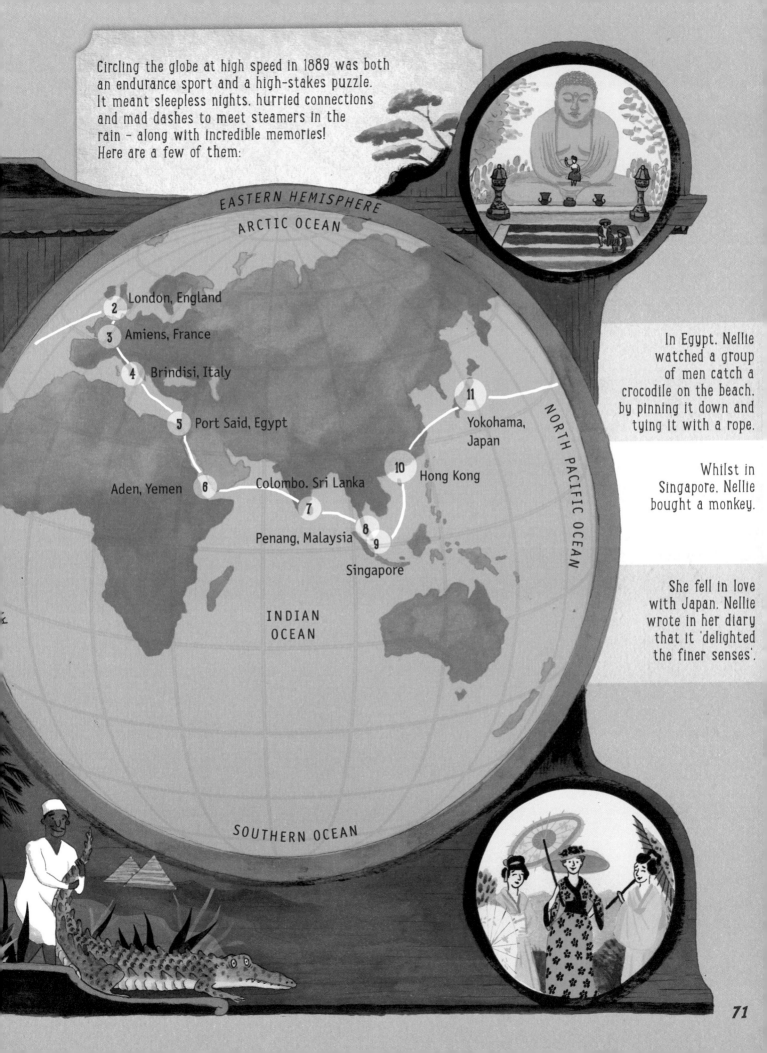

WILFRED THESIGER

Perhaps the last of the great explorers, Wilfred Thesiger strode through the world's wild places. He hated technology and the crowded modern world. Wilfred was happiest when he was far from civilisation in a dangerous landscape. He loved the hardship of desert voyages and the company of desert people, and spent much of his time travelling across Arabia.

Wilfred Thesiger's reputation as one of the greatest modern adventurers was forged after his two epic journeys across the vast Empty Quarter desert on the Arabian Peninsula. It is the largest sand desert in the world and Wilfred crossed it twice by camel. He was supposed to be creating a map of locust migrations for the government, but really he was simply enjoying the challenge of a long journey far from the noisy modern world.

THE BLESSED ONE

While travelling, Wilfred wore local clothes and walked barefoot, just like his Bedu companions – local Arabs who knew the desert well. At times they rode the camels that carried their gear and water, but often they just walked. His two companions could not speak English and called Wilfred 'Mubarak bin London', which is Arabic for 'the blessed one from London'.

THIRSTY WORK

Their diet in the Empty Quarter was extremely basic, limited to flour, dried dates and whatever small animals they could catch. Water was slung over the camels' backs in goatskins which sweated and leaked. This caused great stress as the small group walked through the sands hoping they would come across an oasis where they could refill their water. They often found water only after digging down through the sand, then lowering buckets into the wells to extract the salty water – thirsty work! Can you imagine having to do that in sweltering heat? Often, water was rationed to just half a litre – most people need at least five times that amount in a desert. As a result, Wilfred was tormented by heat and thirst.

SAND AND STARS

At times, Wilfred, bin Kabina and bin Ghabaisha faced great red sand dunes that were up to 30 m high and extremely difficult to cross by camel. Every time a camel slipped or stumbled, they worried that their precious water bags may burst.

At other times, they walked across gravel plains, shimmering in the heat, with an unchanging horizon for day after day – it nearly drove them crazy. On top of all this, Wilfred and his friends were sometimes pursued by tribal raiders. Once, Wilfred was even arrested by the authorities who thought he was a spy!

SWEET RELIEF

Relief came only at nightfall when Wilfred and his companions camped, lighting a tiny fire from the roots of desert plants and kneading flour into dough to bake in the ashes. The men chatted together under the stars, telling stories and sipping tiny cups of strong coffee before wrapping themselves in blankets and sleeping on the hard ground.

KIT

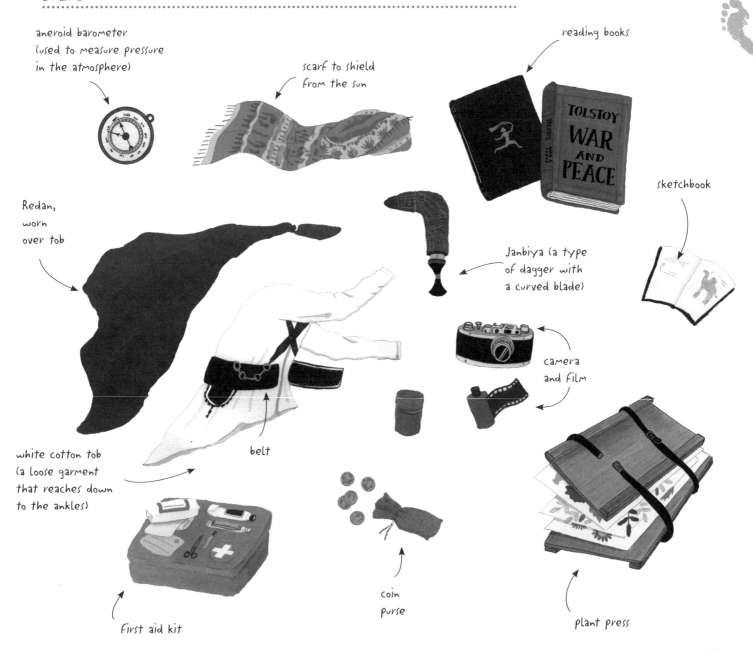

aneroid barometer (used to measure pressure in the atmosphere)

scarf to shield from the sun

reading books

TOLSTOY
WAR
AND
PEACE

sketchbook

Redan, worn over tob

Janbiya (a type of dagger with a curved blade)

white cotton tob (a loose garment that reaches down to the ankles)

belt

camera and film

First aid kit

coin purse

plant press

Why Wilfred Thesiger Inspired Me

I was studying at the same university that Wilfred went to when I read his books. Wilfred had 'the man's courage to live out the boy's dream'. His book, *Arabian Sands,* encouraged me to think ambitiously, but simply, about big journeys of my own. I was inspired to attempt a journey like Wilfred in the scorching, silent sands of the Empty Quarter desert. A decade later, I finally made it happen.

DEAR DIARY

Well, I'm finally coming to the end of the Empty Quarter journey. We have nearly crossed the desert at long last. It seems incredible that it's over.

Sometimes I counted my footsteps to a bush or to some other mark, and it seemed a tiny number compared to how far there still was to go. But I never wanted to go any faster. This way there was time to notice things — a grasshopper under a bush, the tracks of a hare, the shape and colour of ripples on the sand. It would have been very boring to have rushed about in a car.

It has been very hard though. Every day the sun is scorching hot. I felt sick and dizzy when we struggled up the slopes of the huge dunes, climbing through knee-deep, soft sand. I was desperately thirsty most days but we had so little water that I knew it would be many awful hours before I got my evening drink.

My Bedu friends are much tougher than me. Bin Kabina and bin Ghabaisha have become dear friends. I could never have done this without them. They've been used to this hard life since they were born — the rationed water, the bread gritty with bits of sand, the blinding glare and the intense heat. They accept the hardships as they've never known any other way, but this cruel land has cast a spell on me, which nowhere else on Earth can match.

Out here I have learned to not take simple things for granted: clean water to drink, food to eat, shelter and a good night's sleep.

So now I have crossed the Empty Quarter. It's not an important journey to anyone else. The map I've made is pretty inaccurate and if I'm being honest, no one is ever likely to use it. So what was the point? It was a personal experience, and the reward will be a drink of clean, tasteless water. I am content with that.

I know that I will never forget this adventure. You can't live this life without changing in some way. Wherever I go, I know that I will carry the memory of the desert. I am a nomad now — always dreaming of moving on to the next journey — and I know that I will always be yearning to return to the Empty Quarter.

Wilfred

AUDREY SUTHERLAND

Every summer for 20 years, Audrey Sutherland explored the rugged coastline of Alaska in her small inflatable kayak. She was not a tall or strong lady, and her 13,000 km of paddling adventures did not begin until her children were grown up and she had more spare time.

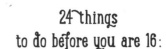

When Audrey Sutherland first set eyes on Alaska, the size of the wilderness and the beautiful islands and bays set her imagination racing. It was totally different to the landscapes of Hawaii where she lived. She began dreaming of a kayak journey around the Alaskan coast. Looking in the mirror one day, she said to herself "Getting older, aren't you, lady? Better do the physical things now. You can work at a desk later." So she quit her job and began planning her first expedition.

> " **What we most regret are not the mistakes we make, but the things we didn't do.** "

LUSCIOUS LANDSCAPES

Over the years, Audrey's journeys took her through some astounding landscapes. She loved the wildlife she saw, such as wolves, bears, salmon and seals. She saw hundreds of whales, and once had a very close encounter with two orcas, which rather frightened her!

One day, Audrey spotted two black fins zooming towards her. She spun her boat around and paddled as fast as she could, but she was headed for a cliff and there was no escape in that direction. Fortunately, the orcas had already passed her and had not been interested in her at all. She scolded herself for being so scared! I wonder if you would have done the same.

The next time Audrey saw an orca, she made herself stay calm as it approached, closer, closer, really close... Her boat lifted with the surge as the killer whale surfaced just a boat's length in front of her, blew air and water, looked at her... then disappeared! She felt dazzled, bewitched and so lucky to have been there!

24 things to do before you are 16:

According to Audrey, every child should be able to:

- Swim 400 m easily
- Do the dishes
- Cook a simple meal
- See work to be done and do it
- Care for tools and always put them away after use
- Splice or put a fixture on an electric cord
- Know basic information about five careers that suit you
- Volunteer to work for a month in each of those fields
- Clean a paintbrush after use
- Change a nappy and a tyre
- Listen to an adult talk with interest and empathy
- Take initiative and responsibility for school work and home chores
- Dance with people of any age
- Clean a fish and dress a chicken
- Know the basic five of first aid: restore breathing and heartbeat, control bleeding, dilute poisons, immobilise fractures, treat for shock
- Read competently
- Write a CV and cover letter
- Know basic car mechanics and simple repairs
- Find your way across a new city using public transport
- Find a paying job and hold it for a month
- Read a map
- Handle a boat safely and competently
- Mend your own clothes
- Do your own laundry

A THOUSAND ISLANDS

Alaska's Inside Passage is a coastal route that winds through more than 1,000 islands of the Alexander Archipelago in southern Alaska. There is a lifetime of adventure in just this one small part of the world – the pristine natural beauty, the long sunsets and the countless perfect camping spots to name but a few.

Audrey spent her winters back home dreaming over maps, plotting and imagining the adventures to come, preparing her food and gear and getting ready for all the surprises that lay in wait the following summer.

Food was an important part of Audrey's adventures. She enjoyed taking the time to cook delicious meals in the wilderness, gathering wild plants and mussels, and cooking them with garlic and olive oil after a long day on the water. Food always tastes better on adventures! Here is one of Audrey's favourite recipes:

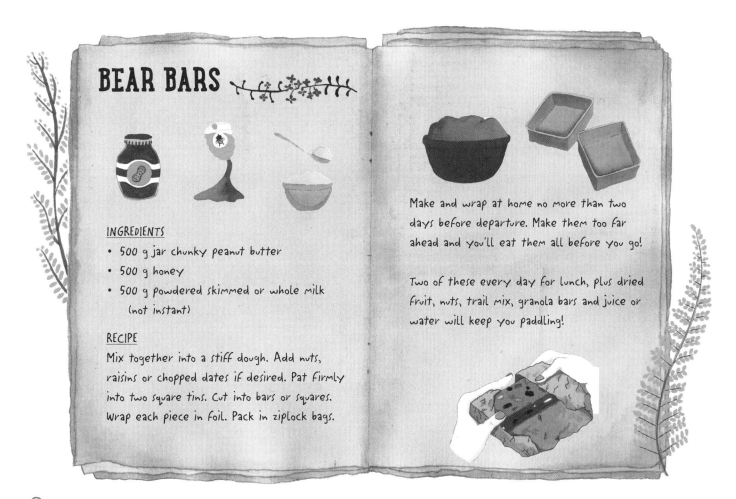

BEAR BARS

INGREDIENTS
- 500 g jar chunky peanut butter
- 500 g honey
- 500 g powdered skimmed or whole milk (not instant)

RECIPE
Mix together into a stiff dough. Add nuts, raisins or chopped dates if desired. Pat firmly into two square tins. Cut into bars or squares. Wrap each piece in foil. Pack in ziplock bags.

Make and wrap at home no more than two days before departure. Make them too far ahead and you'll eat them all before you go!

Two of these every day for lunch, plus dried fruit, nuts, trail mix, granola bars and juice or water will keep you paddling!

Why Audrey Sutherland Inspired Me

Audrey began her adventures later in life. It's a reminder that living adventurously is more about your attitude than your age. Audrey always looked for the best in situations, was honest with herself and did not look for excuses. Most importantly, she remembered to be grateful for the beautiful places she saw, for the adventures she had and for the tasty meals she prepared. Audrey was a great teacher. Her philosophy for adventure was always the same: 'go simple, go solo, go now'.

BENEDICT ALLEN

At just 10 years old, Benedict Allen decided to become an explorer after watching his father, who was a test pilot. Benedict often lives with indigenous people in remote environments and is the only person known to have crossed the Amazon jungle at its widest point. His adventures have taken him across the globe.

Many children dream of being explorers, but as they grow up they are told that the world has already been explored, or that they should get a 'proper job'. But Benedict's dad taught him that there was still an exciting world out there and so he hung on to his dream of becoming an explorer.

AS STRONG AS A CROCODILE

From the Arctic tundra to the wild Amazon jungle, Benedict is one of the most experienced modern explorers. He often spends time with indigenous people, who teach him life-saving skills and sometimes welcome him into their sacred rituals and ceremonies. In this way, Benedict managed to make the first-known crossing of the Amazon Basin at its widest point – a 5,800-km journey on foot that took over seven months to complete.

Amongst other adventures, Benedict spent over five months trekking by horse and camel from Siberia, across Mongolia and the Gobi desert. He also crossed the Namib desert in southern Africa with camels, travelling for three months up the remote Skeleton Coast – named for the whale bones

and shipwrecks washed up on its shore.

On another expedition, Benedict travelled across the icy Bering Strait with only a dog team for company. He is also the only outsider who has been through a tribal ceremony in Papua New Guinea to make him into a 'man as strong as a crocodile'.

GOING SOLO

Without team mates, backup or a mobile phone, Benedict's expeditions are risky and he has been lucky to survive many dangerous situations. Once he even had to sew up his own chest wound with his boot-mending kit and no anaesthetic! Can you imagine doing such a thing? He admits that he has often been afraid on his adventures.

66 My philosophy? In a nutshell, it's about leaving things at home! A GPS, satellite phone and companions – all these things are useful but they limit exposure to the environment that I'm trying to understand. **99**

My name is Benedict and I've had some really scary adventures.

I WAS ONCE ATTACKED BY GREEDY GOLD MINERS, WHO CHASED ME INTO THE FOREST. I HAD TO SURVIVE WITHOUT ANY FOOD OR KIT FOR WEEKS!

I'VE EVEN BEEN SHOT AT BY BANDITS!

ONE TIME, I WAS TRICKED BY MY GUIDES, WHO STOLE ALL MY THINGS AND LEFT ME!

IT'S NOT ALWAYS HUMANS THAT CAUSE BOTHER...

Ok. he's asleep.

Let's go!

MY DOG TEAM RAN AWAY IN A SIBERIAN SNOW STORM. I WOULD HAVE DIED IF I HADN'T SHELTERED IN A SNOW HOLE FOR THE NIGHT.

Every dog for himself!

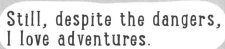

Still, despite the dangers, I love adventures.

All I really need is...

SHELTER AFTER A LONG DAY...

AND SOME SIMPLE FOOD...

Honey ants in the Gibson Desert

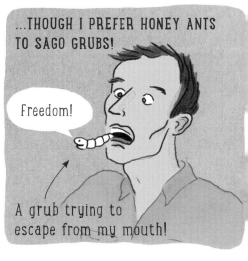

...THOUGH I PREFER HONEY ANTS TO SAGO GRUBS!

Freedom!

A grub trying to escape from my mouth!

KIT

On jungle expeditions, Benedict always carries a survival kit that includes:

1. machete (for cutting through thick vegetation)
2. mustard or ketchup (great for making bugs more tasty!)
3. compass
4. hammock
5. tarpaulin
6. whistle
7. wire
8. hiking boots
9. postcards from home
10. waterproof notepad and pen
11. lighter and waterproof matches
12. fishing hooks

Why Benedict Allen Inspired Me

The first two adventure books I ever read were Ranulph Fiennes' *Living Dangerously* and Benedict Allen's *Mad White Giant*. Both these men became instant heroes to me. In my early years of adventuring, when things went wrong I would often ask myself, "What would Benedict do?" He has tribal tattoos, and has done expeditions in deserts, jungles and the Arctic. He has lived a life filled with adventure. The model adventurer!

SACAGAWEA

A young Native American woman, Sacagawea used her local knowledge to help the famous Lewis and Clark Expedition make the first crossing of what is now the United States. She travelled over 7,000 km with the expedition, by foot, canoe and horse, leading the party through dense forest, raging rivers and steep mountains. What was particularly remarkable is that Sacagawea was only 16 years old and carried her young baby on her back nearly the whole way.

A pregnant Sacagawea meets Lewis and Clark.

Sacagawea has her baby.

The crew's canoe capsizes and Sacagawea saves important documents.

Sacagawea helps with the sale of horses to take the group across the Rocky Mountains.

Sacagawea is reunited with her long-lost brother who is now a chief.

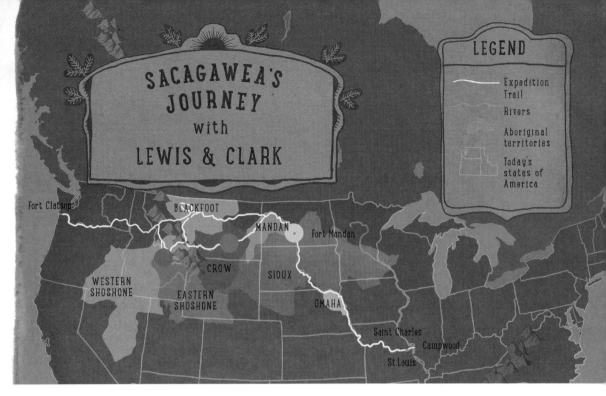

SACAGAWEA'S JOURNEY with LEWIS & CLARK

LEGEND
- Expedition Trail
- Rivers
- Aboriginal territories
- Today's states of America

Fort Clatsop · BLACKFOOT · MANDAN · Fort Mandan · WESTERN SHOSHONE · CROW · EASTERN SHOSHONE · SIOUX · OMAHA · Saint Charles · Campwood · St.Louis

Sacagawea grew up in the Rocky Mountains of Idaho, USA, in the Salmon River region. She belonged to a tribe known as the Lemhi Shoshone Indians.

NEW HORIZONS

Around that time, the young United States of America bought a massive amount of land from France – an area almost nine times bigger than Britain! This new addition meant the country more than doubled in size. However, the new territory had never been explored so two men, Captain Meriwether Lewis and William Clark, were sent on a voyage of discovery. The journey became known as the 'Lewis and Clark Expedition'. They met Sacagawea on the way. Carrying her infant son, she travelled with the group across the new land of America for over a year.

ESSENTIAL SKILLS

Her wide knowledge of roots and vegetables, as well as the local area, proved invaluable to the expedition as Sacagawea knew how to hunt, dig for plants and source food in the remotest of places. Sacagawea was the only Native American, the only woman, the only mother and the only teenager on the trip. At times she must have felt lonely, but being bold and brave, she carried on.

KEEPING CALM

The journey was not without its dangers. The expedition was put in huge peril when the boat the party were travelling on capsized in the Missouri river. But Sacagawea remained calm and saved numerous important documents, instruments, books and medicine that would have otherwise been lost. As a reward for her bravery, Lewis and Clark named that part of the river in her honour and you can still visit it today.

> " Sacagawea has been of great service to me as a pilot through this country. "
> *William Clark*

KIT

The expedition needed to carry a huge variety of equipment. They had kit for travelling in the wilderness, navigating, defence, hunting and fishing, as well as shelter and medical supplies. They also carried many gifts for the Native American tribes they met along the way, including needles, scissors, combs, silk, beads and mirrors.

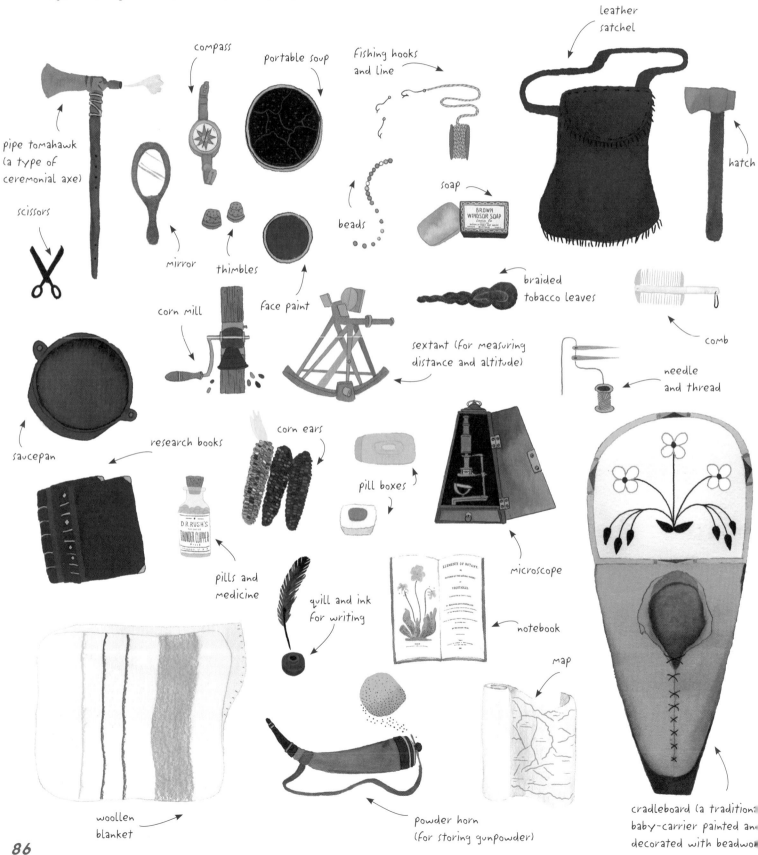

pipe tomahawk
(a type of
ceremonial axe)

scissors

compass

portable soup

fishing hooks
and line

leather
satchel

hatch

soap

BROWN
WINDSOR SOAP

beads

mirror

thimbles

face paint

corn mill

sextant (for measuring
distance and altitude)

braided
tobacco leaves

comb

needle
and thread

saucepan

research books

corn ears

pill boxes

microscope

pills and
medicine

DR. RUSH'S
THUNDER CLAPPER
PILLS

quill and ink
for writing

ELEMENTS OF BOTANY

notebook

map

woollen
blanket

powder horn
(for storing gunpowder)

cradleboard (a tradition
baby-carrier painted an
decorated with beadwo

NATIVE AMERICAN BEEF STEW

INGREDIENTS

- 1 kg cubed buffalo or beef meat
- 50 g butter
- 50 g chopped ham
- 2 tsp crushed garlic
- 1 bay leaf
- 1 finely chopped onion
- 2 sliced carrots
- 800 ml beef stock
- 30 g plain flour
- 2 tbsp chopped fresh parsley
- 1/2 tsp thyme
- salt and pepper to taste

RECIPE

1) In a pan, brown the beef cubes in butter on a high heat. Then add the ham and garlic.
2) Add the bay leaf, onion, carrot and beef stock. Boil until soft.
3) Bring to the boil and simmer for about an hour.
4) Add the flour and stir until the stew starts to thicken.
5) Mix in the parsley, thyme and butter.
6) Remove from the heat, add salt and pepper to taste, and serve.

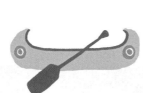

Why Sacagawea Inspired Me

Explorers used to boast of discovering new places, but they often merely visited places where local people had lived quietly for centuries. Sacagawea was not a professional explorer. She was a teenage girl and a young mum. But her people, the Shoshone tribe, had expert knowledge of their land. Sacagawea was a brave and resourceful young person and became an important member of a famous expedition.

THOR HEYERDAHL

Without any sailing experience, and unable to swim,
Thor Heyerdahl was spurred on by simple determination.
He believed that ancient people made long sea voyages before
the invention of navigation tools, and the island people of the
South Pacific could have arrived by boat from South America –
but experts dismissed his theory. To prove them wrong,
Thor decided to replicate the journey.

Kon-Tiki Expedition

KIT

1. potatoes
2. coconuts
3. calabash (a type of fruit)
4. machetes
5. bamboo (to store water)
6. stove
7. sextant
8. harpoon
9. Spanish-speaking parrot

Setting sail from Peru, the men aboard the Kon-Tiki drifted across the Pacific Ocean to the Polynesian Islands, led by Captain Thor Heyerdahl, who named the raft after the Inca sun god. They were at sea on their handmade raft for 101 days.

ANCIENT RAFT

Thor believed that people from South America could have settled in Polynesia by sailing, even though no one else thought the same. He built the Kon-Tiki only using materials that were available to the original raft-building ancient people, including massive balsa wood logs, natural hemp ropes and a cabin roof shaded with huge banana leaves. The crew also carried scientific instruments to collect weather and ocean information and a modern radio, in case of emergency. However, the radio would have been little help calling for rescue given their remote location.

CRASH LANDING

The team sailed almost 7,000 km before smashing into a reef in the Tuamotu Islands. Despite the bumpy arrival, they had successfully made landfall and were all alive and well. Thor had done it!

> **" Borders? I have never seen one. But I've heard they exist in the minds of some people. "**

CALLAO, PERU

Crossing Pacific on a wooden raft. Stop. Will you come? Stop. Only guarantee is free trip to South Sea islands and back. Stop.
---Thor

TAP! TAP! TAP!

COMING.
---Torstein

THOR RECRUITED FOUR NORWEGIANS AND A SWEDE TO JOIN THE ADVENTURE. NONE OF THEM COULD SWIM!

Herman

Erik

Knut

Bengt

Torstein

THEY BUILT THE KON-TIKI USING ONLY THE TECHNOLOGY AND MATERIALS AVAILABLE TO PEOPLE OF THE TIME.

Sail decorated with the image of Kon-Tiki, the Inca sun god

mast

roof of banana leaves

bamboo cabin

balsa wood logs from the Ecuadorian jungle

hemp ropes

LOADED WITH SUPPLIES, THEY SET SAIL, TAKING A SPANISH-SPEAKING PARROT ALONG FOR COMPANY.

¡Adios, amigos!

THE RAFT GROANED AND CREAKED AND DRIFTED THROUGH GOOD WEATHER...

...AND BAD.

SEAWEED AND SHELLFISH GREW ON THE RAFT'S UNDERSIDE, ATTRACTING SARDINES, TUNA AND DOLPHINS.

EACH MORNING, THE COOK COLLECTED FLYING FISH THAT HAD FLOPPED ONTO THE DECK OVERNIGHT.

ONE DAY, A 10-METRE WHALE SHARK CIRCLED THEM FOR AN HOUR BEFORE MOVING ON.

AFTER 93 DAYS, THEY SPOTTED PALM TREES.

LAND AHOY!

MORE THAN A WEEK LATER, THEY SPOTTED A REEF AT DAWN.

BUT THE CURRENT KEPT THEM STUCK OUT AT SEA.

AT LAST THE RAFT RAN AGROUND ON A REEF. WAVES CRASHED OVER THEM AND THE RAFT SNAPPED. BUT THEY HAD MADE IT SUCCESSFULLY TO LAND!

We did it! That'll show everyone!

Why Thor Heyerdahl Inspired Me

Thank goodness for stories like the Kon-Tiki! Everyone told Thor that he was mad. When I began planning adventures of my own, I encountered many people who liked to tell me that things were impossible. Some people who have never done anything exciting urge you not to do anything exciting with your own life. Don't let them stop you – get going!

THE NEXT GREAT ADVENTURER

I hope these explorers have inspired you in their own individual ways, whether it's to learn a new skill, visit a new place or push yourself to the limit. If you are thinking of embarking on your own adventure when you are older, why not dream about where you want to go, what you hope to acheive, how you might travel and what you might need? Remember to let someone know what you are planning and where you are going. This space in the book is for you to dream, to plan, to begin. Will you become the next Great Adventurer?

WHERE WILL YOU GO?

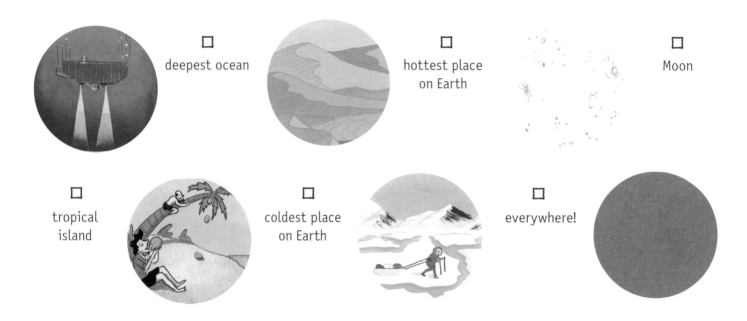

☐ deepest ocean

☐ hottest place on Earth

☐ Moon

☐ tropical island

☐ coldest place on Earth

☐ everywhere!

WHO WILL JOIN YOU?

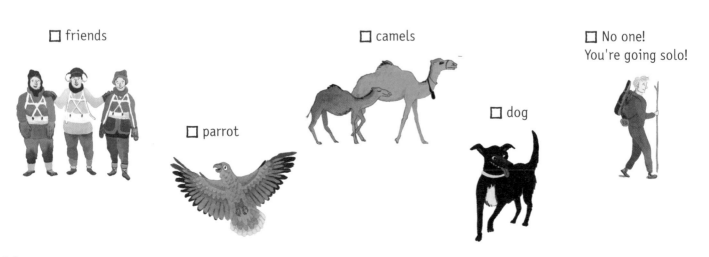

☐ friends

☐ parrot

☐ camels

☐ dog

☐ No one! You're going solo!

WHAT WILL YOU NEED?

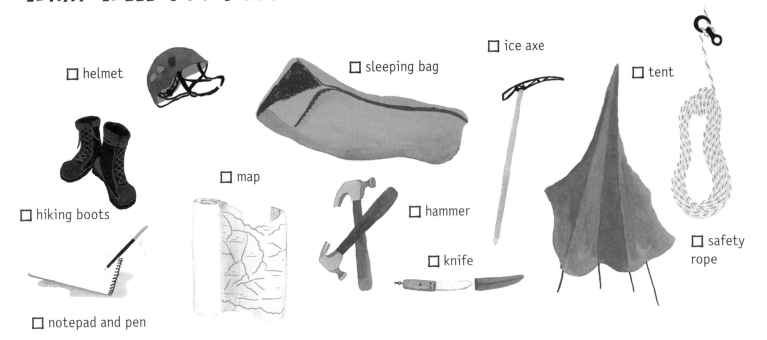

- ☐ helmet
- ☐ ice axe
- ☐ sleeping bag
- ☐ tent
- ☐ hiking boots
- ☐ map
- ☐ hammer
- ☐ knife
- ☐ safety rope
- ☐ notepad and pen

HOW WILL YOU GET THERE?

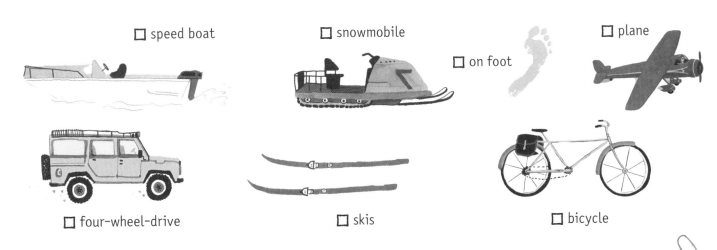

- ☐ speed boat
- ☐ snowmobile
- ☐ on foot
- ☐ plane
- ☐ four-wheel-drive
- ☐ skis
- ☐ bicycle

WHO ELSE WILL INSPIRE YOU?

Mark Pollock
The first blind man to race to the South Pole.

Hillary and Tenzing
The first people to reach the highest point on Earth.

Ernest Shackleton
Ernest led three expeditions to the Antarctic.

Freya Stark
A British-Italian explorer who visited the Middle East.

Thomas Stevens
The first person to cycle round the world on a penny farthing.

Helen Sharman
The first woman to visit the International Space Station.

Marco Polo
One of the most famous explorers of all time.

The Niño Brothers
Four African brothers who sailed with Christopher Columbus on many of his voyages.